English Idioms

Copyright © 2024 Dr. J.M. Saunders. All rights reserved. No part of this publication may be reproduced, distributed, or transmitted in any form or by any means, including photocopying, recording, or 1 other electronic or mechanical methods, without the prior written permission of the author, except in the case of brief quotations embodied in critical reviews and certain other noncommercial uses permitted 2 by copyright law. Teachers may make photocopies of excerpts for classroom use.

About the Author

Dr. J.M. Saunders is a native English speaker and an experienced ESL teacher with a passion for language and linguistics. Having taught English in Costa Rica and Colombia, he truly understands the unique challenges that language learners face, especially when it comes to idiomatic expressions. Recognizing the need for a comprehensive resource, Dr. Saunders authored "English Idioms Origins & Meanings: Book for English Lovers and Learners" to help both ESL students and language enthusiasts gain a deeper understanding of the English language.

Dr. Saunders holds a PhD in English Language Learning and has a strong educational background with a BS in Adult Education and Training and an MBA focused on Performance Improvement. He's a member of the TESOL International Association and also holds a TEFL/TESOL certificate from the International TEFL Academy in Heredia, Costa Rica.

When he's not immersed in the world of teaching and linguistics, Dr. Saunders loves to travel and explore different cultures, which enriches his understanding of language and communication even further.

I hope this book provides you hours of fun and knowledge while entertaining you.

If you enjoy this book, please consider taking 2 minutes to leave a review. I would greatly appreciate it. You can scan the QR code below and it will take you straight to the review page.

Contents

A 1

A Chip Off the Old Block 1

A Dime a Dozen 1

A Dish Fit for the Gods 2

A Firm Hand 2

A Dish Fit for the Gods 3

A Forlorn Hope 3

A Hatchet Job 4

A King's Ransom 4

A Little Bird Told Me 5

A Man's Man 5

A Pain in the Neck 6

A Prince of a Fellow 6

A Snail's Pace 7

A Stone's Throw Away 8

A Tangled Web 8

Abandon Ship 9

Ace in the Hole / Up the Sleeve 9

Achilles' Heel 10

Across the Board 10

Add Another String to One's Bow 11

Against All Odds 11

Against the Clock 12

Against the Grain 12

All's Fair in Love and War 13

An Axe to Grind 14

An Eager Beaver 14

An Honest Broker 15

Another Day, Another Dollar 15

Ants in One's Pants 16

Armchair Expert 16

As Easy as ABC 17

At One's Wit's End 17

B 19

Bad Egg 19

Ball and Chain 19

Bare Bones 20

Barking up the Wrong Tree 21

Be All Thumbs 21

Be on the Lookout 22

Beat Around the Bush 22

Beat Me to the Punch 23

Been There, Done That 24

Beneath One's Dignity 24

Better Late Than Never 25

Between a Rock and a Hard Place 25

Big Fish in a Small Pond 26

Bigger Fish to Fry 26

Bite Off More Than One Can Chew 27

Black and White 28

Black Hole 28

Blaze a Trail 29

Blood Money 29

Blow a Fuse 30

Blow Off Steam 30

Blowing Smoke 31

Break of Dawn 32

Break Open 32

Break the Ice 32

Break the Mold 33

Brownie Points 33

Brush Up On 34

Building Blocks 34

Bull-headed 35

Burn the Midnight Oil 36

Burst One's Bubble 36

By and Large 37

C 38

Call It a Day 38

Call the Shots.. 38

Can't Carry a Tune in a Bucket 39

Can't Teach an Old Dog New Tricks 40

Cat Got Your Tongue 40

Change Gear... 41

Charmed Life.. 41

Cheek by Jowl 42

Chicken Scratches 42

Chopped Liver 43

Clear the Decks 43

Close but No Cigar 44

Cloud of Suspicion 44

Cold Sweat... 45

Come Out Swinging... 46

Coming Out of the Woodwork.. 46

Cool as a Cucumber.. 47

Craft a Narrative 47

Cross One's Fingers 48

Cry Wolf... 48

Cut a Deal.. 49

Cut Someone Some Slack... 49

Cut to the Quick.. 50

D 51

Daggers Drawn 51

- Day In and Day Out 51
- Dead on One's Feet 52
- Delusions of Grandeur 52
- Die with One's Boots On 53
- Dig One's Heels In 53
- Doggy Bag 54
- Don't Have a Leg to Stand On 54
- Don't Put All Your Eggs in One Basket 55
- Double Cross 55
- Down and Out 56
- Down the Hatch 56
- Drag One's Feet 57
- Draw a Blank 57
- Dressed to the Nines 58
- Drive Someone Up the Wall 58
- Drum Up 59

E 60

- Early Bird 60
- Eat Humble Pie 60
- Egg on One's Face 61
- Enter the Lion's Den 61
- Every Rose Has Its Thorns 62
- Eye of a Needle 62

F 64

Facing a Strong Headwind 64
Fall from Grace.. 64
Fall into Place 65
Fall through the Cracks 66
Fast Track Something.. 66
Feeding Frenzy 67
Feeling Groggy 67
Feeling Under the Weather.. 68
Fifty-Fifty... 68
Fight Tooth and Nail 69
Find Your Feet... 69
Fit as a Fiddle 70
Fits the Bill.. 70
Fly the Nest... 71
Flying High 71
Fool's Gold.. 72
Fools Rush In 72
Fresh as a Daisy... 73
Fun and Games Until Someone Loses an Eye 73

G 75

Game Plan 75
Get a Kick Out of Something.. 75
Get a Life 76
Get Cold Feet.. 77

x

Get Down to Business 77
Get Off One's High Horse 78
Get Off Scot-Free 78
Get on a Soapbox 79
Get Out of Dodge 80
Get Someone's Goat 80
Get the Lead Out 81
Get Under One's Skin 81
Get Wind of 82
Getting Hitched 82
Give a Leg Up 83
Glass Ceiling 84
Gnash One's Teeth 84
Go the Extra Mile 85
Go the Whole Nine Yards 85
Good Samaritan 86
Goody Two-Shoes 87
Got It in the Bag 87
Graveyard Shift 88
Gray Area 89
Grin and Bear It 90

H 91
Happy as a Lark 91
Hard and Fast 91

Hard Nut to Crack 92

Have One Foot in the Grave 92

Have One's Heart Set on Something 93

Have Someone Over a Barrel 94

Have the Last Laugh 94

Have Your Cake and Eat It Too 95

Head off at the Pass 95

Head on a Platter 96

Heads Up 97

Heart Is in the Right Place 97

Hedge Your Bets 98

Hell Bent 99

Hit the Hay 99

Hold on for Dear Life 100

Hold One's Tongue 100

Hold the Fort 101

Hold Your Horses 102

Hook, Line, and Sinker 102

I 104

If the Creek Don't Rise 104

In a Pickle 104

In Broad Daylight 105

In Deep Waters 105

In for a Penny, In for a Pound 106

In High Spirits 107

In One's Neck of the Woods 107

In Seventh Heaven 108

In the Black/Red 108

In the Dark 109

Isn't Over Till the Fat Lady Sings 110

It's All Greek to Me 110

J 112

Jekyll and Hyde 112

Jump for Joy 113

Jump to Conclusions 113

K 115

Keep a Stiff Upper Lip 115

Keep One's Head Above Water 116

Keep One's Shirt On 116

Keep Pace 117

Keep Someone on Their Toes 118

Keep Under One's Hat 118

Knee High to a Grasshopper 119

Knock It out of the Park 119

Knock One's Socks Off 120

Knowledge Is Power 121

Knuckle Down 122

L 123

Land on One's Feet 123

Lead Someone by the Nose 123

Leaps and Bounds 124

Leave Someone to Their Own Devices 125

Lend a Hand 125

Let Someone Have It 126

Let the Cat Out of the Bag 126

Life in the Fast Lane 127

Life Is a Bowl of Cherries 128

Lighten Up 129

Lightning Never Strikes Twice 129

Like a Broken Record 130

Like Death Warmed Over 130

Like Taking Candy from a Baby 131

Like Water off a Duck's Back 131

Live and Let Live 132

Live on a Shoestring 133

Living on Borrowed Time 133

Long Shot 134

Look Daggers at 135

Look What the Cat Dragged In 135

Loose Cannon 136

Loose Lips Sink Ships 137

Lose Your Marbles 137

Lost in Thought 138
Lower the Bar 139
Lower Your Guard 139

M 141
Magic Bullet 141
Make Someone's Blood Boil 141
Middle of the Road 142
Monkey See, Monkey Do 142

N 144
No Pain, No Gain 144
No Time Like the Present 144
Not for All the Tea in China 145
Not My Cup of Tea 146
Not on My Watch 146
Not the Sharpest Pencil in the Box 147
Not the Sharpest Tool in the Shed 147
Not to Mince One's Words 148

O 149
Off the Beaten Track 149
Off the Record 150
Old Enough to Know Better 150
Old Flame 151
Old School/Skool 151
On Cloud Nine 152

On Hand 153

On Pins and Needles 153

On the Right Track 154

On the Same Wavelength 154

On Thin Ice 155

One for the Road 156

Out in the Open 156

Out of Line 157

Out of the Gate 157

Over the Moon 158

P 159

Paint the Town Red 159

Paper Tiger 160

Pass with Flying Colors 160

Pay Lip Service 161

Pecking Order 162

Phone Ringing Off the Hook 163

Pie in the Sky 163

Pipe Down 164

Play Hard to Get 164

Play to the Gallery 165

Pot Calling the Kettle Black 166

Prick Up One's Ears 166

Pros and Cons 167

Pull One out of the Hat 168

Pull the Plug 168

Pushing up Daisies.. 169

Put a Spoke in Someone's Wheel.. 169

Put One's Thinking Cap on 170

R 171

Rain on Someone's Parade 171

Raise the Bar 171

Raring to Go... 172

Read the Riot Act 173

Red Herring 173

Rest Assured 174

Resting on One's Laurels 174

Ride Out the Storm... 175

Right off the Bat 176

Rip off the Band-Aid 176

Rome Wasn't Built in a Day 177

Rough It 177

Rub Elbows With 178

Rubber Check... 178

Rule the Roost 179

Run Amuck 179

Run of the Mill 180

S... 181

xvii

Save One's Bacon 181
Saving for a Rainy Day 181
Scratch My Back and I'll Scratch Yours 182
Sea Change 183
See a Man About a Dog 183
Sell Like Hotcakes 184
Set off on the Right/Wrong Foot 185
Settle Down 185
Shipshape 186
Short Shrift 187
Show Someone the Door 187
Silver Bullet 188
Silver Lining 189
Sink One's Teeth into Something 189
Sitting Pretty 190
Skeleton in the Closet 190
Sleeping with the Enemy 191
Smell Something Fishy 192
Snake in the Grass 192
Snowed Under 193
Son of a Gun 193
Spellbound 194
Spit It Out 194
Stand One's Ground 195

Start from Scratch 195

Step Up to the Plate 196

Stick One's Neck Out 196

Stir the Hornet's Nest 196

Straight from the Horse's Mouth 197

Straight Shooter 197

Stubborn as a Mule 198

Sunny Disposition 198

Sweat Like a Pig 199

T 200

Tail Between One's Legs 200

Take a Load Off 200

Take Five 201

Take Someone to the Cleaners 201

Take Something Out on Someone 201

Take the Cake 202

Taken Aback 202

Talk Someone into Something 203

Taste of One's Own Medicine 203

Test the Waters 203

That's the Way the Ball Bounces 204

The Apple Doesn't Fall Far from the Tree 204

The Big Picture 204

The Chips Are Down 205

The Golden Age 205

The Jig is Up 206

The Lion's Share 206

The Middle of Nowhere 206

The Upper Crust 207

The World is Your Oyster 207

There's the Rub 208

Thick as Thieves 208

Thinking Outside the Box 208

Through Thick and Thin 209

Throw Down the Gauntlet 209

Throw Someone to the Lions 210

Throwing Shade 210

Tick Off 210

Tight as a Tick 211

Till the Cows Come Home 211

To Bandy Something About 212

To Be in Someone's Black Book 212

To Be Left High and Dry 212

To Blackball 213

To Bury the Hatchet 213

To Give the Cold Shoulder 214

To Let One's Hair Down 214

To Pull Someone's Leg 214

To the Moon and Back 215

Tongue in Cheek 215

Toss Up 215

Tree Hugger 216

Tug at One's Heartstrings 216

Turn a Blind Eye 217

Turn the Other Cheek 217

Twist of Fate 217

U 219

Under Siege 219

Up the Ante 219

Upper Hand 220

Upset the Apple Cart 220

Us and Them 220

Use Your Noodle 221

W 222

Way to Go 222

Weight off One's Shoulders 222

Wet Behind the Ears 223

Wet Blanket 223

Win-Win Situation 223

Wise Beyond One's Years 224

With Bells On 224

Workhorse 224

Worth One's Salt 225

Wreak Havoc 225

Y 226

Yes Man 226

Yoke Around One's Neck 226

Z 227

Zero Hour 227

Zero Tolerance 227

Zip One's Lip 228

A

A Chip Off the Old Block

Meaning: A person who looks or acts like one of their parents.

Origin: Imagine a young soldier training with his father in ancient Rome. The young soldier wants to be like his father, so he copies his father's moves. He fights just like his father, showing their strong family bond. The poet Theocritus described a son who was like his father in his Idylls. Just like a small piece of stone is similar to the larger block it was cut from, the son is like his father.

In English, this phrase became popular in the 17th century as "chip of the old block."

Example: Mark won the same sailboat race his father won twenty years ago; he's a chip off the old block.

A Dime a Dozen

Meaning: Something so common that it has little value.

Origin: Imagine you are at a busy market on vacation. There are many stalls with the same trinkets and souvenirs. A dozen of these items can be bought for just a dime, showing they are not special. This is the idea behind the phrase "a dime a dozen."

Example: Plastic toys like this are a dime a dozen.

A Dish Fit for the Gods

Meaning: An offering of exceptional quality.

Origin: Imagine a grand banquet hall with rich, regal tapestries and the warm glow of candlelight. On long, polished tables, a magnificent feast is laid out—each dish a dazzling work of culinary art, as if made by the gods themselves. This is the essence of the phrase "a dish fit for the gods"—food that goes beyond mere sustenance, celebrating the chef's craft. The phrase comes from Shakespeare's Julius Caesar, where Brutus, in thinking about Caesar's fate, suggests honoring the fallen ruler like an offering to the gods.

Example: The chef's signature dessert was truly a dish fit for the gods.

A Firm Hand

Meaning: Strong, unwavering discipline and control.

Origin: The phrase "a firm hand" has been used since the 16th century to symbolize strong control and discipline. "Firm" suggests something solid and unyielding, showing strength, resolve, and authority. This idiom describes a strict and decisive approach to managing people or situations. Whether it's a parent guiding a child with steady discipline or a leader directing a team with clear decisions, a "firm hand" means having the strength to lead and protect.

Example: Children need a firm hand growing up—they crave structure and rules, even if they protest.

A Dish Fit for the Gods

Meaning: An offering of exceptional quality.

Origin: Imagine a grand banquet hall with rich, regal tapestries and the warm glow of candlelight. On long, polished tables, a magnificent feast is laid out—each dish a dazzling work of culinary art, as if made by the gods themselves. This is the essence of the phrase "a dish fit for the gods"—food that goes beyond mere sustenance, celebrating the chef's craft. The phrase comes from Shakespeare's Julius Caesar, where Brutus, in thinking about Caesar's fate, suggests honoring the fallen ruler like an offering to the gods.

Example: The chef's signature dessert was truly a dish fit for the gods.

A Forlorn Hope

Meaning: A desperate or extremely difficult task.

Origin: The term "forlorn hope" comes from the Dutch phrase verloren hoop, which means "lost troop." It was used to describe a group of soldiers sent on the most dangerous missions, often the first to attack or face a risky task with little chance of survival. These soldiers knew they were likely to fail, but they still went forward. Over time, the phrase has come to mean any task or effort that seems almost impossible, where success feels out of reach and the chances of winning are very small.

Example: Embarking on the startup venture felt like a forlorn hope, given the fierce competition and market uncertainties.

A Hatchet Job

Meaning: A forceful or malicious verbal attack.

Origin: In a busy newsroom in the early 20th century, reporters rushed to meet deadlines while editors barked orders. Amidst the chaos, one journalist, armed with a sharp pen and a quick mind, was tasked with writing a scathing review. He didn't hold back—his words cut through the subject with the precision of a hatchet, tearing apart every flaw, leaving little room for sympathy. This is how the phrase "hatchet job" came to be, inspired by the image of a small axe used for chopping. It was meant to describe a quick, forceful action, much like a harsh, unforgiving criticism. By the 1940s, the expression had become common, often referring to criticisms that were not just harsh but unfair, designed to destroy rather than to help.

Example: The journalist's review was a hatchet job, leaving no praise for the author's work.

A King's Ransom

Meaning: An extremely large sum of money.

Origin: In the 14th century, during a chaotic battle, King John II of France was captured by the English. His captors, knowing the immense value of a king, demanded a ransom so large that it could bankrupt entire nations. The sum required for his release was a "king's ransom," a fortune beyond belief. This event gave birth to the expression, originally referring to the vast amounts of money needed to free a captured monarch. Over time, the phrase evolved to describe any large sum of money, a fortune considered extravagant by most standards.

Example: The rare painting was sold for a king's ransom at the auction.

A Little Bird Told Me

Meaning: An expression used to indicate that the speaker has received information from an undisclosed or secret source.

Origin: The phrase "a little bird told me", can be traced back to the Book of Ecclesiastes in the Old Testament. In Ecclesiastes 10:20, it says, "Do not revile the king even in your thoughts, or curse the rich in your bedroom, because a bird in the sky may carry your words; a bird on the wing may report what you say." This passage warns that even private conversations can be overheard, much like a bird carrying a secret message. Over time, the expression evolved into the more playful and colloquial "a little bird told me", used to humorously suggest that the speaker knows something but keeps the source of their information a mystery.

Example: "How did you know about the surprise party?" "A little bird told me."

A Man's Man

Meaning: An individual who embodies traditionally masculine traits and is admired by other men for his strength, toughness, or charm.

Origin: In the 19th century, the phrase "a man's man" was used to describe a man who earned the respect of other men. Imagine life on the rugged frontier, where a man had to be strong, independent, and tough to survive. Those who showed these qualities were called "a man's man." It meant they were admired for their strength, leadership, and ability to handle difficult challenges. Over time, the phrase has expanded, but it still describes someone who has qualities that other men admire and respect.

Example: He was always the first to step up and take charge, truly a man's man in every sense.

A Pain in the Neck

Meaning: An expression used to describe someone or something that is particularly annoying or troublesome.

Origin: The phrase "a pain in the neck" dates back to the early 20th century. Imagine someone sitting at a desk for hours, their neck stiff and aching, forcing them to stop and rub the sore spot. The discomfort is annoying—not serious, but it refuses to be ignored. Over time, people started comparing this small but persistent pain to other frustrations in life. Whether it was a task they didn't want to do or a person who kept bothering them, they began saying, "What a pain in the neck!" The phrase stuck, and now we use it to describe anything—or anyone—that gets on our nerves.

Example: Dealing with constant technical issues at work has become a real pain in the neck.

A Prince of a Fellow

Meaning: An expression used to describe a man who is exceptionally admirable, generous, or outstanding in character.

Origin: The term "prince of a fellow" has been in use since at least 1864, inspired by the image of a prince—not merely a figure of royalty, but a symbol of nobility, honor, and kindness. Picture a man in a bustling 19th-century town square, tipping his hat with a warm smile as he helps a stranger load heavy goods into a wagon. His actions stand out, not for grandeur but for genuine decency, earning him admiration from everyone around.

This phrase captures the essence of someone who embodies the highest virtues—a person who is generous, reliable, and admired by all who know him. Over time, "prince of a fellow" became a way to describe individuals who inspire respect and affection through their character, not their status. It reminds us that true nobility comes from how we treat others, making the term just as meaningful today as it was then.

Example: John is a prince of a fellow; he always goes out of his way to help others.

A Snail's Pace

Meaning: An extremely slow speed or rate.

Origin: The expression "a snail's pace" has been around since the 15th century, inspired by the famously slow movement of snails. Imagine watching a snail make its way across a garden path, its tiny body inching forward so slowly that you could mark its progress by the shifting shadows. This image perfectly captures the frustration of waiting for something that moves far too slowly, whether it's a long line, a delayed project, or a slow conversation. Over the centuries, "a snail's pace" has remained a timeless way to describe anything that drags on endlessly.

Example: The traffic was moving at a snail's pace during the rush hour.

A Stone's Throw Away

Meaning: An expression indicating a very short distance.

Origin: The phrase "a stone's throw away" has been in use since at least the 16th century. Imagine a smooth, rounded stone, launched with a swift, practiced motion, arcing through the air before settling gently on the ground. This image of a stone's throw signifies a brief journey across the landscape. The term "stone's throw" defines a short distance that can be easily covered, and the addition of "away" emphasizes the nearness of the destination. It's a phrase that conjures a sense of immediacy, a promise of a destination just beyond the horizon.

Example: The park is just a stone's throw away from my house.

A Tangled Web

Meaning: An intricate and complicated situation, often resulting from deceit or dishonesty.

Origin: "O, what a tangled web we weave, when first we practice to deceive!" This haunting line from Sir Walter Scott's epic poem, Marmion, warns about the dangerous nature of deceit. It paints a picture of a confusing maze, a complex network of lies and half-truths that traps its creator. When we start deceiving, we create a tangled web, each lie adding more complexity. As the web grows, it becomes harder to untangle, and the consequences become more severe. The phrase reminds us that honesty is the best policy and the only path to true freedom.

Example: His lies created a tangled web that was difficult to untangle.

Abandon Ship

Meaning: An order given to evacuate a ship because it is sinking or in imminent danger.

Origin: "Abandon ship!" A chilling cry from the perilous seas, echoing through the ages. For centuries, these words have meant imminent danger, uttered by captains facing the reality of a sinking vessel. Steeped in maritime tradition, the phrase signifies desperation and finality. It reminds us of the dangers of seafaring and the courage of those who brave the open waters. Abandoning a ship is a desperate measure, a recognition that survival lies in escape, not resistance.

Example: When the startup's funding dried up and key investors pulled out, the Founder had no choice but to abandon ship and shut down operations.

Ace in the Hole / Up the Sleeve

Meaning: A hidden advantage or resource kept in reserve until needed.

Origin: An ace in the hole, a hidden gem, a secret weapon. This phrase comes from the high-stakes world of poker. In stud poker, players conceal a single card, a mystery card that could be a king, a queen, or, most importantly, an ace. This hidden card, the ace in the hole, offers a strategic edge, potentially changing the game's outcome. Over time, this poker term has become a part of everyday language, referring to any concealed advantage or secret weapon that can be used at the right moment. Whether it's a surprise talent, a hidden resource, or a well-kept secret, an ace in the hole can be a powerful tool for success. It reminds us that sometimes, the most valuable assets are those that remain unseen until needed.

Example: His extensive network of contacts was his ace in the hole during the negotiations.

Achilles' Heel

Meaning: A weakness or vulnerable point in someone or something that is otherwise strong or invulnerable.

Origin: According to legend, the mighty warrior Achilles was dipped into the River Styx by his mother, Thetis, to make him invulnerable. However, she neglected to immerse his heel, leaving it vulnerable. This oversight proved to be Achilles' downfall. During the Trojan War, a poisoned arrow struck his heel, causing a fatal wound. Thus, the phrase "Achilles' heel" has come to symbolize a weakness or vulnerability, a fatal flaw that can bring down even the strongest of heroes. It serves as a reminder that no one is invincible and that even the strongest can be undone by their own weaknesses.

Example: Chocolate is my Achilles' heel; I just can't resist it.

Across the Board

Meaning: Applying to all categories, individuals, or aspects in a given situation.

Origin: The phrase "across the board" comes from the high-stakes world of horse racing. In horse racing, a bet placed "across the board" means a wager on a horse to win, place, or show, covering all three possible outcomes. This term has found its way into everyday language to describe a broad approach that considers all angles. Whether it's a business strategy, a political campaign, or a personal endeavor, an across-the-board approach seeks to address all relevant factors, leaving no stone unturned. It aims to maximize potential outcomes by considering all possibilities.

Example: The new policy applies across the board, meaning everyone will be affected.

Add Another String to One's Bow

Meaning: To acquire an additional skill or resource, expanding one's abilities or options.

Origin: The phrase "add another string to one's bow" comes from the ancient art of archery. In archery, having a spare string is crucial, as it ensures the archer can continue shooting even if the primary string breaks. Over time, this practical concept has evolved into a metaphor, signifying the value of acquiring additional skills and talents. Just as an extra string enhances an archer's capabilities, a diverse skill set increases an individual's chances of success. It reminds us that versatility is a valuable asset, and by learning new things, we can better prepare ourselves to face challenges and seize opportunities.

Example: She's learned web design, adding another string to her bow in the competitive job market.

Against All Odds

Meaning: Despite very difficult or unlikely circumstances.

Origin: The phrase comes from the world of gambling, where "odds" refer to the probability of an event happening. "Against all odds" is a phrase that defies expectation, showcasing the power of the human spirit. It encapsulates the thrill of defying probability and achieving the impossible. In the realm of chance and uncertainty, where odds are calculated, the phrase signifies a remarkable feat and a triumph over adversity.

Example: The team managed to win the championship against all odds, after a series of setbacks.

Against the Clock

Meaning: Doing something under pressure, often with a strict deadline.

Origin: "Time is of the essence," a ticking clock that pushes us forward, urging us to seize the moment. This phrase captures the urgency of time and the relentless march of seconds, minutes, and hours. It evokes the image of a sand timer, with grains slipping through, reminding us of time's fleeting nature. When time is of the essence, every moment counts, and the pressure can drive us to push our limits and achieve extraordinary feats. It reminds us that procrastination is a luxury we can't afford and that success often depends on timely action.

Example: We were racing against the clock to finish the project before the deadline.

Against the Grain

Meaning: Doing something in a way that is contrary to the usual or expected way, often with effort or resistance.

Origin: "Going against the grain" evokes the image of a craftsman working with wood. The grain of the wood, or the direction of its fibers, is important to consider. Cutting against the grain means to defy the natural order and work against the flow of the material, requiring more effort, skill, and patience. Over time, this term has evolved into a metaphor representing actions that defy convention and challenge the status quo. It celebrates individuality, originality, and the courage to think differently. By going against the grain, we can pave new paths, spark innovation, and create a better future.

Example: Her decision to leave her job and start a business went against the grain of what most people expected.

All's Fair in Love and War

Meaning: In certain situations, any behavior is justified to achieve a desired outcome, especially in love or conflict.

Origin: Love and war, a timeless pairing, are two forces that can consume and transform. This phrase, often attributed to the sixteenth-century English writer John Lyly, captures the intensity and unpredictability of both love and war. In love, emotions run high, passions ignite, and reason often takes a backseat to desire. Similarly, in war, the rules of engagement are suspended, and the pursuit of victory can lead to acts of bravery and brutality. This phrase suggests that love and war share a common thread: a willingness to push boundaries, take risks, and fight for what one believes in. Both can be all-consuming experiences that leave a lasting impact. It is a reminder that the lines between love and war can blur, and that the heart, like the battlefield, can be a dangerous place.

Example: He stole his rival's business plan, but as they say, all's fair in love and war.

An Axe to Grind

Meaning: To have a personal issue or grievance that needs to be addressed.

Origin: The phrase "an axe to grind" dates back to the eighteenth century and evokes the image of a blacksmith sharpening a tool for a specific purpose. It suggests a hidden motive or personal agenda. Popularized by Benjamin Franklin, the phrase paints a picture of someone looking to settle a score or pursue a particular goal. When someone has an axe to grind, they are motivated by personal interest rather than a desire to help or inform. It serves as a reminder to consider others' underlying intentions and be wary of hidden motives.

Example: She's been acting strange ever since the meeting, and I think she has an axe to grind with me.

An Eager Beaver

Meaning: Someone who is enthusiastic, hardworking, and eager to take on tasks.

Origin: The phrase "an eager beaver" is inspired by the industrious nature of beavers. Beavers are known for their tireless efforts in building dams and lodges, symbolizing hard work and dedication. When someone is described as an eager beaver, it means they are constantly striving to achieve their goals, driven, motivated, and always seeking new challenges. This phrase highlights the power of hard work and perseverance, reminding us that diligent effort can lead to great achievements.

Example: Tom's an eager beaver in the office; he always volunteers for extra projects.

An Honest Broker

Meaning: A person who acts fairly and impartially, especially in negotiations or disputes.

Origin: The phrase "an honest broker" dates back to the seventeenth century. It evokes the image of a fair and impartial facilitator, someone who acts with honesty and transparency. In the complex world of finance, law, and diplomacy, an honest broker is highly valued, capable of navigating negotiations and ensuring all parties are treated fairly. This phrase suggests a commitment to ethical behavior and fairness, reminding us that it is possible to find common ground even in contentious situations. An honest broker symbolizes trust, good faith, and positive change.

Example: As an honest broker, she helped mediate the contract without taking sides.

Another Day, Another Dollar

Meaning: A way of expressing that each day's work is just another routine task, usually implying that the work is monotonous or unremarkable.

Origin: The phrase "another day, another dollar" originates from the construction of the Panama Canal, where workers were reportedly paid just one dollar per day for their labor. This signifies a repetitive, mundane job where each day brought the same small amount of money, essentially meaning "just another day of ordinary work." The phrase often carries a hint of resignation, acknowledging that work is a necessary part of life, a sacrifice made to survive. Yet, it also carries a sense of resilience and determination to keep going, no matter how tedious or thankless the task.

Example: Back to the office tomorrow—another day, another dollar.

Ants in One's Pants

Meaning: To be restless, anxious, or unable to stay still.

Origin: The idiom "ants in your pants" originated in the United States, where "pants" refers to underwear. While there is no logical explanation for the idiom's origin, it's easy to imagine someone fidgeting and wiggling if ants or other insects were in their underwear. Whether it's a child bouncing off the walls or an adult pacing nervously, the phrase "ants in one's pants" perfectly captures the feeling of restlessness and the inability to focus or relax. It is a humorous yet accurate way to describe a common human experience, reminding us that sometimes, our bodies and minds simply need to move.

Example: He couldn't sit still during the meeting; he had ants in his pants the whole time.

Armchair Expert

Meaning: Someone who offers opinions or judgments without having direct experience or knowledge of the subject.

Origin: The phrase "armchair expert" comes from the idea of sitting in an armchair, a comfortable, passive position, rather than being actively involved in something. It evokes the image of someone who sits comfortably, offering opinions and advice without firsthand experience. This term carries a sense of condescension, suggesting a lack of practical knowledge and a tendency to theorize without action. Armchair experts are often quick to criticize, slow to praise, and eager to share their uninformed opinions. They may have a lot of book-learning, but they lack real-world skills and experience necessary to truly understand complex situations. By remaining in their comfortable armchairs, they avoid the risks and challenges associated with active participation, preferring to critique from a distance.

Example: He's an armchair expert when it comes to football, but he's never played a day in his life.

As Easy as ABC

Meaning: Something that is very simple or easy to do.

Origin: The phrase "as easy as ABC" is often used to describe tasks that require minimal effort or skill. It provides comforting reassurance that a challenge can be easily overcome. This phrase reminds us that even the most complex problems can be broken down into smaller, manageable steps, making them less daunting and more achievable.

Example: Setting up the new software was as easy as ABC; it only took a few minutes to learn.

At One's Wit's End

Meaning: To be in a state of confusion or frustration, unable to think of a solution.

Origin: The idiom "at one's wit's end" comes from Middle English literature, specifically the poem "Piers Plowman" by William Langland, around the 1300s. In this context, "wit" refers to one's mental faculties. When someone is "at their wit's end," they have exhausted all their mental abilities to solve a problem and are completely perplexed or helpless. This phrase often describes a state of despair or hopelessness, feeling overwhelmed and unable to cope. It reminds us of the limitations of the human mind and that we cannot always solve every problem without help or new knowledge.

Example: After trying every possible fix, I'm at my wit's end with this computer issue.

B

Bad Egg

Meaning: A person who is dishonest, untrustworthy, or behaves in a morally wrong manner.

Origin: A "bad egg" conjures up the image of a spoiled, rotten egg, aptly describing someone who is morally corrupt or socially undesirable. Originating in the United States between 1850 and 1855, this idiom captures the essence of a troublesome, dishonest, or simply unpleasant person. Just as a single bad egg can spoil an entire batch, a "bad egg" can negatively affect those around them. This term often describes individuals who are selfish, manipulative, or destructive, implying a lack of empathy and compassion.

Example: Watch out for him—he's a bad egg and can't be trusted.

Ball and Chain

Meaning: A person or thing that limits one's freedom or progress, often referring to an oppressive responsibility or commitment.

Origin: The idiom "ball and chain" originates from the historical practice of attaching a heavy iron ball to a prisoner's leg with a chain, used as a physical restraint to prevent escape and limit movement. Metaphorically, "ball and chain" refers to anything that restricts one's freedom or ability to act freely. The phrase often describes the feeling of being trapped or weighed down, unable to break free from a situation that no longer serves us. It reminds us that sometimes, the heaviest chains are those we impose upon ourselves, and true freedom comes from breaking free from self-imposed limitations.

Example: "After taking on so many commitments at work, he felt like his job was a ball and chain."

Bare Bones

Meaning: The essential or most basic part of something, with everything else removed or stripped down.

Origin: Shakespeare used the term "bare bone" to refer to a skinny person in 1598, but the first records of "bare bones" referring to the bare essentials come from about 300 years later. This idiom captures the essence of something reduced to its most basic form, devoid of all unnecessary adornment. Just as a skeleton is the bare framework of a living organism, so too can a bare-bones presentation or argument be stripped of all extraneous details, focusing solely on the essential elements. In the modern world, the phrase "bare bones" is often used to describe something that is simple, straightforward, and devoid of complexity. It can refer to a minimalist design, a concise explanation, or a stripped-down version of a product or service. While a bare-bones approach may lack sophistication or elegance, it can be highly effective in conveying a message or achieving a goal.

Example: The project proposal was just the bare bones; we'll add the details later.

Barking up the Wrong Tree

Meaning: To pursue a mistaken or misguided course of action, or to make an incorrect assumption.

Origin: The phrase "barking up the wrong tree" originates from early 19th-century American hunting practices. Hunters would sometimes observe their dogs barking at the base of a tree. However, the prey animal might not actually be in that tree. This led to the idiom, which describes pursuing the wrong course of action or accusing the wrong person. The phrase "barking up the wrong tree" is often used to describe someone who is mistaken, misled, or simply misguided. It is a reminder that it is important to carefully consider our assumptions and to avoid jumping to conclusions. By taking the time to gather information and analyze evidence, we can avoid barking up the wrong tree and focus our energy on more productive pursuits.

Example: I think you're barking up the wrong tree if you think he's responsible for the problem.

Be All Thumbs

Meaning: To be clumsy or awkward with one's hands, often causing mistakes or mishaps.

Origin: The idiom "all thumbs" comes from a proverb in John Heywood's 1546 collection, which states, "When he should get aught, each finger is a thumb." The idiom is used to describe someone who is physically awkward, particularly with their hands. When someone is described as "all thumbs," it often evokes a sense of amusement or sympathy. It is a humorous way to acknowledge a common human failing—the struggle to master physical skills that may come easily to others. While clumsiness can be frustrating, it is also a reminder that everyone has their strengths and weaknesses, and even the most skilled individuals may stumble from time to time.

Example: I'm all thumbs when it comes to assembling furniture — I need some help!

Be on the Lookout

Meaning: To watch carefully for something or someone, typically with the intent of spotting something important or dangerous.

Origin: The phrase "be on the lookout" originates from nautical terminology, where a "lookout" was a person stationed on a ship to watch for potential dangers like other vessels or land. Essentially, it means to be alert and vigilant. In the modern world, the phrase "lookout" is often used as a warning or a call to action. It can be a simple reminder to pay attention, be mindful of one's surroundings, or anticipate potential challenges. By staying alert and vigilant, we can navigate life's uncertainties and avoid unnecessary pitfalls.

Example: Be on the lookout for any suspicious activity while you're walking home.

Beat Around the Bush

Meaning: To avoid addressing a subject directly, often by speaking in vague or evasive terms.

Origin: The phrase "beat around the bush" evokes the image of a hunter, indirectly pursuing their prey. This idiom, with roots in the sixteenth century, captures the essence of indirectness and evasion. Just as a hunter might beat around a bush to flush out a hidden animal, so too can a person avoid direct confrontation or a difficult conversation. The phrase originates from medieval hunting practices, where hunters would employ people to "beat" around bushes with sticks to scare out game animals, essentially avoiding directly hitting the bushes themselves. This symbolizes the act of approaching a topic indirectly or avoiding the main point of a conversation.

Example: Stop beating around the bush and tell me what you really think about the proposal.

Beat Me to the Punch

Meaning: To act before someone else can, usually by getting to a goal or achieving something first.

Origin: The phrase "beat you to the punch" comes from boxing, where "punch" refers to a strong blow. "Beating someone to the punch" means landing the first significant blow, effectively winning the fight by acting before your opponent does. Thus, "beat me to the punch" means someone did something before you had the chance to do it yourself. The phrase is often used to describe a situation where someone has taken advantage of an opportunity before you or has stolen your thunder by announcing a plan or idea first. It is a reminder that in a competitive world, speed and decisiveness are often rewarded.

Example: I was planning to ask for a promotion, but my colleague beat me to the punch and got the promotion instead.

Been There, Done That

Meaning: To have experienced something already, and thus, not be interested in it anymore.

Origin: The phrase "been there, done that" evokes a sense of familiarity and experience. Popularized in the mid-twentieth century, it captures the feeling of having already encountered a particular situation or completed a specific task. It suggests indifference or boredom, as if the experience has lost its novelty or excitement. When someone says "been there, done that," they signal that they have nothing new to learn or contribute. It can be a dismissive response, indicating a lack of interest or enthusiasm, but it can also humorously acknowledge a shared experience or convey a sense of world-weariness.

Example: "You want to try skydiving? Been there, done that – I'm not looking for that thrill again."

Beneath One's Dignity

Meaning: To be considered too low or humiliating for someone of a certain status or self-respect.

Origin: The phrase "beneath one's dignity" comes from the Latin phrase infrā dignitātem, which is shortened to "infra dig". The word "dignity" comes from the Latin word dignus, which means "worth" or "value". When someone says something is beneath their dignity, they are asserting their superiority and rejecting the idea of stooping to such a level. This phrase often carries a connotation of arrogance or snobbery, implying a belief in one's own importance and the inferiority of others.

Example: She refused to pick up the trash; it was beneath her dignity as the company's CEO.

Better Late Than Never

Meaning: It is better to do something late than to not do it at all.

Origin: The phrase "better late than never" originates from the Latin phrase "potiusque sero quam nunquam," which directly translates to "rather late than never." The first recorded use of this expression in English is found in Geoffrey Chaucer's "The Canterbury Tales." By reminding us that it's never too late to make a change or pursue a goal, this phrase inspires us to overcome procrastination and seize the day, no matter how late it may seem.

Example: He didn't go to college until he was 30, but better late than never.

Between a Rock and a Hard Place

Meaning: To be faced with two difficult or undesirable choices, with no easy solution.

Origin: "Between a rock and a hard place" evokes the image of a perilous predicament, a situation where any choice leads to a difficult or dangerous outcome. This idiom is rooted in Greek mythology, where Odysseus must navigate between Scylla, a monstrous creature on a cliff (the rock), and Charybdis, a dangerous whirlpool (the hard place). This concept signifies a situation with no good options, where choosing either side leads to a difficult outcome; it is often attributed to Homer's Odyssey. When someone finds themselves between a rock and a hard place, they are faced with a dilemma, requiring careful consideration and strategic thinking, as any choice made may have significant consequences.

Example: I'm stuck between a rock and a hard place—either I accept the new job with less pay or stay in my current position with no chance for growth.

Big Fish in a Small Pond

Meaning: A person who is important or influential within a small or limited group or environment.

Origin: "Big fish in a small pond" evokes the image of a powerful entity in a limited domain. This idiom, with roots in the sixteenth century, captures the idea of relative importance, suggesting that one's significance can be magnified or diminished depending on the context. A big fish in a small pond holds a dominant position in a limited environment, influential or powerful within a specific group or community. However, when placed in a larger context, their influence may diminish. This phrase reminds us that perceived importance is often relative and true greatness is measured by the quality of one's actions and the impact one makes on the world.

Example: He's a big fish in a small pond at the local law firm, but he's just one of many lawyers at the national level.

Bigger Fish to Fry

Meaning: To have more important things to do or concerns to address than the current issue.

Origin: "Bigger fish to fry" evokes the image of a fisherman prioritizing larger catches over smaller ones. This idiom, with roots in the seventeenth century, captures the idea of focusing on more important matters and setting aside less significant tasks for more pressing concerns. When someone says they have bigger fish to fry, they are indicating that they have more important things to do. This phrase is often used to politely decline a request or excuse oneself from a less important task. It reminds us that time is a valuable resource and it is important to prioritize our efforts and focus on what truly matters.

Example: I can't worry about this minor issue right now; I've got bigger fish to fry with the upcoming project.

Bite Off More Than One Can Chew

Meaning: To take on more responsibility or tasks than one can handle.

Origin: "Bite off more than you can chew" evokes the image of a gluttonous individual attempting to consume more than their appetite can handle. This idiom, with roots in the early nineteenth century, captures the essence of overreaching, of taking on a task or challenge that is beyond one's capacity. When someone bites off more than they can chew, they are likely to experience difficulty, stress, and even failure. This phrase reminds us of the importance of setting realistic goals and avoiding overextending ourselves. By taking on manageable tasks and pacing ourselves, we can increase our chances of success and reduce the risk of burnout.

Example: I bit off more than I could chew when I agreed to run both the marketing and sales departments.

Black and White

Meaning: Clear, simple, and unambiguous; easy to understand or distinguish.

Origin: The phrase "black and white" originated in the Middle English period (1150–1500). Just as the colors black and white represent the extremes of the color spectrum, so too does the phrase signify the extremes of a situation. When something is described as "black and white," it means that there is no room for interpretation or ambiguity. It is a clear-cut issue, a straightforward decision, a simple truth. The phrase often emphasizes the importance of honesty, transparency, and direct communication.

Example: The rules are black and white—if you're late, you're disqualified.

Black Hole

Meaning: A situation or place into which things disappear or are lost, often with no way out.

Origin: "Black hole" is a term that evokes images of cosmic mystery and infinite darkness. It was originally coined in 1968 by Princeton physicist John Archibald Wheeler. Wheeler credited an audience member for suggesting the term during a lecture in New York City in December 1967, as they were tired of hearing him repeatedly say "gravitationally completely collapsed object." Just as a celestial black hole devours matter and energy, a figurative black hole can absorb time, money, or emotional energy. It can represent a project, relationship, or habit that drains one's resources without providing any tangible benefit.

Example: The new department has become a black hole for our budget—no matter how much money we throw at it, it never seems to get better.

Blaze a Trail

Meaning: To be a pioneer by doing something innovative or untested, often paving the way for others.

Origin: "Blaze a trail" originated in the mid-1770s to describe the practice of marking trees with notches or chips in the bark to indicate a trail in the forest. The term is still used today and can also be used figuratively to mean finding a new path or method, or beginning a new undertaking. Just as a pioneer blazes a trail through the forest, creating a path for future travelers, an individual or group can blaze a trail in their chosen field, breaking new ground and setting new standards. This phrase reminds us of the importance of taking risks, challenging the status quo, and forging our own paths.

Example: She's blazing a trail in the tech industry with her innovative ideas.

Blood Money

Meaning: Money paid in compensation for a life lost or obtained through unethical means.

Origin: In the Christian Bible, Judas Iscariot received 30 pieces of silver in exchange for revealing Jesus Christ's identity to the Pharisees. After the crucifixion, Judas returned the money to the chief priests, who called it "the price of blood." The phrase "blood money" often describes money obtained through criminal activities, such as extortion, bribery, or drug trafficking. It can also refer to compensation paid to victims of crime, especially when a life has been lost or someone has been seriously injured. The term carries strong moral condemnation, highlighting the destructive and harmful consequences of such actions.

Example: The journalist refused to accept what he described as blood money for promoting a harmful product.

Blow a Fuse

Meaning: To lose one's temper suddenly and become very angry.

Origin: The idiom "blow a fuse" comes from the literal function of an electrical fuse, which "blows" (melts) when too much electricity flows through it, effectively breaking the circuit to prevent damage. Metaphorically, it represents a sudden and intense outburst of anger when someone is pushed beyond their limit, like an overloaded electrical circuit. When someone blows a fuse, they may exhibit a range of emotional responses, from mild annoyance to outright rage. This phrase reminds us of the importance of managing our emotions and responding to stress in a healthy and constructive way.

Example: When he saw the dent in his car, he blew a fuse.

Blow Off Steam

Meaning: To release pent-up energy or emotions, often through physical activity or by expressing oneself.

Origin: The idiom "blow off steam" originates from the mechanics of old steam engines, where excess pressure in the boiler would be released by opening a valve, essentially "blowing off" the steam to prevent the engine from exploding. Metaphorically, it represents the release of pent-up emotions or energy by engaging in an activity to relieve stress. Just as a steam engine releases pressure to avoid damage, we can release our pent-up emotions to prevent them from boiling over. This phrase highlights the importance of finding healthy ways to express our feelings and manage stress. Whether it's through physical activity, creative pursuits, or simply talking to a friend, finding an outlet for our emotions can help us maintain our mental and emotional well-being.

Example: After a stressful week, she went for a long run to blow off steam.

Blowing Smoke

Meaning: To mislead, deceive, or speak without sincerity; to boast or exaggerate without intending to act.

Origin: The idiom "blowing smoke" originates from the practice of magicians using smoke to obscure their sleight of hand tricks, effectively deceiving the audience by creating a visual distraction. Metaphorically, it means to mislead or exaggerate something to hide the truth, often by using empty words or boasts. When someone is blowing smoke, they are likely engaging in empty rhetoric, making promises they have no intention of keeping, or exaggerating their abilities or achievements. This phrase reminds us of the importance of honesty, transparency, and authenticity in our interactions with others.

Example: He claims he'll double our salaries, but I think he's just blowing smoke.

Break of Dawn

Meaning: The very first light of day; sunrise.

Origin: This idiom has been used since at least the 16th century to describe the moment when the first light appears in the sky, signaling the beginning of the day.

Example: We set out on our hike at the break of dawn to catch the sunrise.

Break Open

Meaning: To force something open; to open something violently or forcefully.

Origin: "Break open" evokes the image of force and destruction, of barriers being shattered and boundaries being breached. It signifies a forceful action, a violent separation, a breaking free from constraints.

Example: The firefighters had to break open the door to rescue the trapped occupants.

Break the Ice

Meaning: To initiate conversation in a social setting; to overcome initial social awkwardness.

Origin: The idiom "break the ice" originates from the nautical practice of using special ships called "icebreakers" to navigate through frozen waters by breaking through the ice, creating a path for other larger ships to follow. Metaphorically, it represents the act of initiating a conversation or social interaction in a new or potentially awkward situation by doing something to ease tension and make others feel more comfortable. When we break the ice, we create a more comfortable and welcoming atmosphere, encouraging others to participate and engage in conversation. By initiating a conversation, sharing a story, or simply smiling, we can help to alleviate social awkwardness and foster a sense of community.

Example: To break the ice at the meeting, he told a humorous anecdote.

Break the Mold

Meaning: To do something in a completely new way, deviating from established patterns or traditions.

Origin: This phrase originates from the manufacturing process, where a mold is used to create identical copies of an object. To "break the mold" means to destroy the form, ensuring that no further identical items can be produced. Metaphorically, it symbolizes uniqueness, innovation, and a departure from conventional norms. It implies doing something in a new and unconventional way, challenging the status quo, and setting a new standard.

Example: Her innovative approach to teaching really breaks the mold of traditional education methods.

Brownie Points

Meaning: Imaginary credit awarded for doing good deeds or earning favor, often through flattery or pleasing actions.

Origin: The phrase "brownie points" originates from the "Brownies," a junior group within the Girl Scouts who earn points or rewards for completing good deeds, essentially meaning "credit for doing something helpful." Thus, "brownie points" refers to gaining favor by performing positive actions; the term is most commonly associated with the Girl Scouts system.

Example: He's been working late every day to earn brownie points with the boss.

Brush Up On

Meaning: To improve or refresh one's knowledge or skills in a particular area.

Origin: The phrase "brush up on" is believed to originate from the idea of lightly "brushing" away dust or dirt to refresh something, metaphorically representing the act of quickly reviewing or improving a skill or knowledge that might have become slightly dull due to disuse. The earliest recorded usage of "brush up" dates back to around 1600. When we brush up on a skill or subject, we are taking the time to review and reinforce our understanding. We are polishing our knowledge, sharpening our abilities, and preparing ourselves for new challenges. This phrase highlights the importance of lifelong learning and the value of continuous improvement.

Example: Before traveling to France, she decided to brush up on her French.

Building Blocks

Meaning: The basic components or elements that form the foundation of something.

Origin: "Building blocks" evokes the image of a child constructing a castle or tower, piece by piece. This metaphor, rooted in the simplicity of childhood play, captures the essence of fundamental elements that form the foundation of something more complex. In various contexts, from education to business to personal development, building blocks represent the essential skills, knowledge, or experiences necessary for growth and progress. By understanding and mastering these foundational elements, we can build a strong and stable foundation for our future endeavors.

Example: Understanding grammar is one of the essential building blocks of mastering a new language.

Bull-headed

Meaning: Stubborn; determined to do what one wants without considering others' opinions or feelings.

Origin: "Bull-headed" evokes the image of a stubborn bull, charging forward without regard for obstacles or diversions. This idiom, with roots in the animal kingdom, captures the essence of obstinacy and the refusal to yield or compromise. When someone is described as bull-headed, it means they are determined to have their own way, regardless of the consequences. They are resistant to reason, unwilling to listen to others' perspectives, and often prone to acting impulsively. This phrase reminds us of the importance of flexibility, compromise, and open-mindedness.

Example: He's so bull-headed; once he makes up his mind, there's no changing it.

Burn the Midnight Oil

Meaning: To work late into the night, often past usual working hours, to accomplish a task.

Origin: "Burning the midnight oil" originates from the practice of using oil lamps for light at night before electricity was widely available. It essentially means someone is working so late that they are literally "burning oil" to stay illuminated through the night hours, signifying late-night work or studying. Just as the oil in a lamp is consumed as it burns, so too is our energy depleted when we work late into the night. This phrase reminds us of the importance of balance, the need to rest and recharge. While it is sometimes necessary to work late to meet a deadline or complete a project, it is important to avoid burning the midnight oil too often, as it can lead to fatigue, stress, and burnout.

Example: With the deadline approaching, she had to burn the midnight oil to finish the project on time.

Burst One's Bubble

Meaning: To shatter someone's illusions or destroy their sense of happiness by revealing an unpleasant truth.

Origin: "Burst one's bubble" evokes the image of a delicate soap bubble, ready to burst at the slightest touch. This idiom captures the essence of shattering someone's illusions, dispelling a comforting fantasy with a harsh reality. Just as a bubble can be popped, so too can a person's optimistic beliefs be shattered by a sudden revelation or harsh truth. When someone bursts another's bubble, they are often seen as being cruel or insensitive. However, it is important to remember that honesty, even when painful, can be a valuable gift. By confronting difficult truths, we can avoid future disappointment and make more informed decisions.

Example: I hate to burst your bubble, but the concert was canceled due to the storm.

By and Large

Meaning: Generally speaking; for the most part.

Origin: The idiom "by and large" originates from nautical terminology, specifically referring to a ship's ability to sail both "by the wind" (close to the wind's direction) and "large" (with the wind hitting the broadside of the ship). It essentially means it can handle different wind directions and sail well in most conditions; thus, "by and large" came to mean "generally" or "on the whole" in everyday language. When we use the phrase "by and large," we acknowledge the complexities of a situation and the existence of both positive and negative aspects. It is a way of taking a holistic view, considering the overall picture rather than focusing on specific details.

Example: By and large, the conference was a success, despite a few technical issues.

C

Call It a Day

Meaning: To stop working on something, especially for the rest of the day.

Origin: The idiom "call it a day" originates from the earlier phrase "call it half a day," which meant to leave work before the workday was fully over, first recorded around 1838. Essentially, deciding to stop working early and "call it a day" evolved from this concept of leaving before the day was completely finished. Just as a worker might call it a day after a long shift, we can use this phrase to signify the conclusion of any undertaking, whether it's a work project, a study session, or a recreational activity. It acknowledges the completion of a task and signals the beginning of a new phase.

Example: We've made good progress; let's call it a day and continue tomorrow.

Call the Shots

Meaning: To be in control or make the important decisions.

Origin: "Call the shots" comes from the idea of a marksman in military training, where if they successfully hit a target, they would "call the shot," meaning they would announce their accurate aim. Essentially, it signifies that they are in control and making the decisions. When someone calls the shots, they are the ultimate decision-maker, the person with the power to influence the course of events. This phrase is often used to describe individuals who hold positions of authority, such as CEOs, politicians, or coaches. It highlights the importance of strong leadership and the ability to make tough decisions.

Example: As the project manager, it's your job to call the shots and ensure everything runs smoothly.

Can't Carry a Tune in a Bucket

Meaning: A humorous way of saying someone is completely tone-deaf or cannot sing well at all.

Origin: "Can't carry a tune in a bucket" is a humorous phrase that paints a vivid picture of someone who is utterly tone-deaf. Likely rooted in folk humor, this idiom captures the essence of someone who is completely incapable of singing on key. The imagery of a bucket filled with tunes, spilling and leaking due to a person's poor singing, is both comical and evocative. This phrase is often used to describe someone who sings so badly that it is painful to listen to. It is a playful way of acknowledging a common human flaw—the inability to sing well. While some people are blessed with natural musical talent, others may struggle to carry a tune, no matter how hard they try.

Example: My brother loves karaoke, but honestly, he can't carry a tune in a bucket.

Can't Teach an Old Dog New Tricks

Meaning: It's difficult to teach new habits or skills to someone who is set in their ways.

Origin: The idiom "can't teach an old dog new tricks" originates from a 16th-century English proverb, first appearing in print in a book called "The Boke of Husbandry" by John Fitzherbert. It was used literally to describe the difficulty of training older dogs to perform new tricks, essentially meaning it's hard to change established habits in old age. Just as an old dog may struggle to learn new commands, older people can find it challenging to adopt new habits or embrace new technologies. This phrase reminds us that while experience and wisdom are valuable assets, they can sometimes hinder our ability to adapt to change.

Example: Trying to get my grandfather to use a smartphone is impossible—you can't teach an old dog new tricks.

Cat Got Your Tongue

Meaning: Used to ask someone why they are silent or not responding.

Origin: "Cat got your tongue?" is a playful phrase with mysterious origins. One theory suggests a connection to the "cat-o'-nine-tails," a whip used to punish sailors in the 18th century, silencing even the most vocal. Another theory posits that ancient rulers punished those who displeased them by having their tongues removed and fed to cats. Regardless of the specific origin, the phrase has evolved into a lighthearted way to prod someone into speaking, reminding us that silence can sometimes be more powerful than words. Playful banter often breaks the ice and encourages conversation.

Example: You've been awfully quiet since the meeting started. What's the matter—cat got your tongue?

Change Gear

Meaning: To adjust or shift focus, pace, or method of doing something.

Origin: This phrase originates from driving, where shifting gears allows a vehicle to adjust its speed and power. Picture a race car driver smoothly shifting gears to navigate a winding track or accelerate on a straight stretch. This image of adaptability and flexibility has extended to the metaphorical use of the phrase. In everyday language, "change gears" means to alter one's approach or strategy, implying a shift in focus, a change in direction, or a modification in behavior. For example, a person might "change gears" in a conversation, moving from a casual topic to a more serious one. Or, a business might "change gears" to adapt to a new market trend.

Example: We'll need to change gear and move faster if we want to meet the deadline.

Charmed Life

Meaning: A life that seems unusually blessed with good fortune or protection.

Origin: A phrase steeped in the magic of storytelling, "charmed life" evokes the image of a person seemingly protected by a benevolent force. It conjures visions of a life untouched by misfortune, blessed with extraordinary luck. The phrase often carries a sense of wonder and envy, as if the person were living a fairy tale. Rooted in ancient beliefs in magic and superstition, the term has its origins in literature and mythology. Shakespeare's *Macbeth* famously used the phrase to describe his perceived invincibility. This literary reference has solidified the phrase's association with a life seemingly protected by a higher power, immune to ordinary trials and tribulations.

Example: Despite the challenges, she's always had a charmed life, finding success at every turn.

Cheek by Jowl

Meaning: Very close together, either physically or in relationship to.

Origin: This evocative phrase paints a vivid picture of close proximity. It conjures images of a crowded market, a bustling city street, or a packed subway car, where people are pressed together, almost touching cheek to jowl. Rooted in Old English, the phrase originated in the 16th century. The earliest known use of the phrase was in 1577 in a translation by Meredith Hanmer, a historian and clergyman for the Church of England and Church of Ireland. The phrase means to be close together or side by side.

Example: The houses in this old neighborhood are built cheek by jowl.

Chicken Scratches

Meaning: Messy or illegible handwriting.

Origin: "Chicken scratches" is a vivid phrase that paints a picture of messy, illegible handwriting. It conjures the image of a chicken scratching at the ground, leaving behind a chaotic pattern of lines and curves. This imagery perfectly captures the appearance of hastily written or poorly formed script. The phrase is often used humorously to describe someone's poor handwriting or a hastily written note. It highlights the contrast between a clear, legible script and one that is difficult to decipher.

Example: I can barely read these notes—your handwriting looks like chicken scratches!

Chopped Liver

Meaning: Something or someone considered unimportant or overlooked.

Origin: This idiom, rooted in Jewish culinary traditions, paints a picture of being overlooked or undervalued. It conjures the image of a humble side dish, often overshadowed by the main course. Chopped liver, though delicious in its own right, is often seen as a secondary dish, a supporting player rather than the star of the show. Metaphorically, being "chopped liver" means being disregarded or treated as insignificant. It implies a feeling of being overlooked, undervalued, or taken for granted. This phrase is often used to express frustration or disappointment, particularly when one feels their contributions or opinions are not being recognized or appreciated.

Example: When everyone praised her colleague and ignored her, she felt like chopped liver.

Clear the Decks

Meaning: To prepare for action by removing unnecessary items or distractions.

Origin: This maritime phrase originates from naval warfare, where it meant to prepare for battle by removing or securing all loose objects on the ship's deck, essentially getting ready for action by clearing away potential obstacles. This act of preparation, of clearing away distractions, has evolved into a metaphor for readiness and focus. Today, we use "clear the decks" to mean preparing for a significant task or challenge. It implies a need to eliminate distractions, prioritize tasks, and focus on the essential. Whether it's a major project at work, a big exam, or a personal goal, clearing the decks allows us to approach the challenge with a clear mind and a focused effort.

Example: Let's clear the decks before we start brainstorming ideas for the new campaign.

Close but No Cigar

Meaning: To almost succeed but fall short at the last moment.

Origin: This colorful phrase paints a vivid picture of carnivals and fairs in the late 19th century, where the prize for winning a game was often a cigar. If someone came close to winning but missed, the carnival barker would shout "close, but no cigar" to indicate they didn't win the prize. It's a reminder that life is often filled with near-misses, moments where success seems within reach yet slips through our fingers. While the phrase might sound a bit harsh, it can also be a source of motivation, encouraging us to strive for greater accuracy and persistence in our endeavors.

Example: We almost won the game, it was close but no cigar.

Cloud of Suspicion

Meaning: A state of doubt or mistrust hanging over someone.

Origin: This evocative phrase paints a picture of doubt and mistrust, like a dark cloud hanging over a person's reputation. It suggests a sense of uncertainty and the feeling that something is amiss. The image of a literal cloud, often associated with storms and uncertainty, is a powerful metaphor for the intangible nature of suspicion. When someone is under a cloud of suspicion, they are seen with distrust and skepticism, their actions and motives questioned. This can significantly impact their social and professional life, damaging their reputation and eroding trust.

Example: Despite the evidence, he was still under a cloud of suspicion.

Cold Sweat

Meaning: A sudden feeling of fear or anxiety accompanied by sweating.

Origin: "Cold sweat" is a vivid phrase that paints a picture of intense fear or anxiety. It captures the physical sensation of sweating, often accompanied by chills, that occurs during moments of high stress. The paradox of feeling cold while sweating is a unique characteristic of this physiological response. The phrase likely originated from the physiological response to fear, where the body's "fight or flight" response triggers the release of adrenaline, causing increased sweating even in cold environments. This physical sensation has been used metaphorically to describe intense emotional states like fear, anxiety, or nervousness.

Example: The thought of speaking in public brought a cold sweat to her brow.

Come Out Swinging

Meaning: To start or react to something with strength and force.

Origin: This idiom originates from boxing, where it refers to a fighter who starts a round or match by immediately throwing punches aggressively, essentially "coming out" with a strong, forceful attack right from the beginning. It implies a vigorous and immediate response to a challenge or situation. The phrase highlights the importance of a strong and decisive response, especially when faced with adversity. It suggests that by taking the offensive, one can gain a psychological advantage and increase their chances of success.

Example: When the company faced criticism, the CEO came out swinging in its defense.

Coming Out of the Woodwork

Meaning: To appear suddenly, often to take advantage of an opportunity or reveal an opinion. It can also mean to appear after being hidden or inactive for a long time.

Origin: The phrase "coming out of the woodwork" originates from the idea of insects, like termites or cockroaches, suddenly appearing from hidden places within the woodwork of a house. It signifies someone or something emerging unexpectedly from obscurity or seclusion after being unnoticed for a while. Ultimately, this idiom serves as a reminder that sometimes, things that we least expect can emerge from the shadows.

Example: As soon as she won the lottery, long-lost relatives started coming out of the woodwork.

Cool as a Cucumber

Meaning: To be calm, composed, and untroubled, especially in stressful situations.

Origin: "As cool as a cucumber" is a phrase that evokes the image of a refreshing vegetable, remaining calm and collected in the face of adversity. This idiom, with roots in the eighteenth century, captures the essence of composure and self-control. Cucumbers, renowned for their cool, soothing properties, are a fitting metaphor for a person who remains unruffled, even in the most stressful of circumstances. It means someone is very calm and relaxed, even in a stressful situation. They don't get nervous or upset easily. They can think clearly, act decisively, and remain calm under pressure. This phrase is a testament to the power of self-control, a reminder that by staying calm and focused, we can navigate life's challenges with grace and confidence.

Example: Even during the intense negotiations, he was as cool as a cucumber and never showed signs of stress.

Craft a Narrative

Meaning: To create a story or explanation to influence or persuade others.

Origin: The phrase "craft a narrative" originates from the word "craft," meaning "skillful creation," and "narrative," meaning "story." It signifies the act of carefully constructing a story with deliberate techniques and attention to detail, much like a skilled artisan would craft an object. "Craft" comes from the Old English word "craeft," which means "strength" or "skill." In the modern world, crafting a narrative is a powerful tool used in various fields, from marketing and advertising to politics and journalism. By carefully constructing a compelling narrative, individuals and organizations can shape public opinion, inspire action, and achieve their goals.

Example: By crafting a narrative that resonated with voters, the politician was able to win the election.

Cross One's Fingers

Meaning: To hope for good luck or a positive outcome.

Origin: The phrase "cross one's fingers" originates from an ancient superstition where crossing your fingers resembled the shape of a Christian cross, symbolizing a plea for good luck or divine intervention. This practice gained particular traction in 16th-century England, where people crossed their fingers to ward off evil and ill health.

Example: She crossed her fingers, hoping to win the contest.

Cry Wolf

Meaning: To give a false alarm or lie repeatedly, leading others to distrust future claims.

Origin: This idiom, rooted in Aesop's fable, paints a vivid picture of a person who repeatedly raises false alarms, only to be ignored when a genuine crisis arises. The image of a shepherd boy crying "wolf" for fun, only to be met with disbelief when a real wolf attacks the flock, is a powerful metaphor for the consequences of dishonesty and exaggeration.

Example: If you keep crying wolf, no one will believe you when it really matters.

Cut a Deal

Meaning: To negotiate and reach an agreement.

Origin: This idiom likely comes from the idea of "cutting" away parts of your offer during a negotiation, like slicing a piece of something until both sides are happy. It's like you're slowly "cutting" down to a deal that works for everyone. When people "cut a deal," they are essentially collaborating to find a mutually beneficial solution. It requires skill, diplomacy, and a willingness to compromise.

Example: The company cut a deal to acquire the startup.

Cut Someone Some Slack

Meaning: To be lenient or give someone a break, especially in difficult circumstances.

Origin: This phrase is believed to originate from the nautical term "slack," which refers to loose or extra rope on a ship. Essentially, "cutting some slack" means to loosen the rope, giving someone more room to maneuver. When we "cut someone some slack," we are showing compassion and understanding, recognizing their limitations and offering them a break. This phrase often encourages empathy and tolerance, reminding us that everyone makes mistakes and deserves a second chance.

Example: I know she's late again, but her schedule has been hectic — cut her some slack.

Cut to the Quick

Meaning: To hurt someone deeply, especially emotionally.

Origin: This vivid phrase paints a picture of deep emotional pain. It conjures the image of a physical wound, a sharp cut that penetrates the skin and reaches the sensitive flesh beneath. This metaphor highlights the intense emotional impact of words or actions that can wound a person's feelings. The phrase "cut to the quick" originates from the old meaning of the word "quick," which means "living" or "alive," essentially referring to the sensitive, living flesh under a fingernail. "Cutting to the quick" means to deeply hurt or wound someone, like piercing the tender flesh under the nail with a sharp object, implying a sharp, deep emotional pain.

Example: Her harsh criticism cut him to the quick, leaving him speechless.

D

Daggers Drawn

Meaning: To be on the verge of an intense argument or conflict.

Origin: This evocative phrase paints a vivid picture of intense hostility and conflict. It conjures the image of two adversaries, each poised to strike with a deadly weapon. The imagery of drawn daggers, ready to inflict harm, highlights the tension and animosity between the parties involved. The phrase is often used to describe a situation where two people or groups are on the brink of a serious argument or confrontation. It suggests a high level of animosity and a potential for violence.

Example: After the heated debate, the two politicians had daggers drawn, neither willing to back down from their position.

Day In and Day Out

Meaning: To consistently perform the same actions or tasks over an extended period.

Origin: This phrase evokes the image of a monotonous routine, a repetitive cycle of actions that occurs consistently over time. It conjures the feeling of a never-ending cycle, where the same tasks are performed day after day. This phrase is often used to describe jobs that require consistent effort and attention, such as factory work or customer service. It can also describe personal habits or routines, such as daily exercise or meditation. The phrase emphasizes the persistence and dedication required to maintain a consistent pattern of behavior.

Example: He's been working on that project day in and day out for weeks.

Dead on One's Feet

Meaning: Extremely tired or exhausted but still continuing to function.

Origin: "Dead on your feet" is a phrase that vividly captures the feeling of extreme exhaustion while still pushing through tasks or responsibilities. It conjures the image of someone so tired that they can barely stand, yet they continue to move forward. This idiom is often used to describe situations where people are physically and mentally drained, but still manage to carry on due to their commitment or necessity.

Example: After working a double shift, she was dead on her feet but still managed to finish her assignments.

Delusions of Grandeur

Meaning: An exaggerated sense of one's importance, power, or abilities.

Origin: The term "delusions of grandeur" originated from an incident involving brothers Henry and Stephen Prouse Cooper. Henry was investigated for insanity after publicly declaring in court that he was a grand person. The phrase is commonly used to describe individuals who have an exaggerated sense of their own abilities, importance, or power. They may believe they have special powers, talents, or knowledge that others lack. This can manifest in various ways, such as grandiose plans, extravagant claims, or a sense of entitlement.

Example: His delusions of grandeur made him think he could run the company with no experience.

Die with One's Boots On

Meaning: To keep working or living actively until the very end.

Origin: The phrase means to die while still actively engaged in one's work or profession. This phrase often carries a sense of honor and respect, as it suggests a life well-lived. It can be used to describe someone who works tirelessly until the very end, refusing to slow down or retire. This idiom is a reminder of the importance of living life to the fullest, pursuing our dreams and passions with unwavering dedication.

Example: He was a dedicated doctor and vowed to die with his boots on, helping patients until his last breath.

Dig One's Heels In

Meaning: To refuse to change your position or opinion, despite pressure.

Origin: This phrase evokes the image of stubborn resistance. It conjures the picture of an animal, such as a horse or mule, planting its hooves firmly into the ground, refusing to budge. This metaphor describes a person determined to resist change or pressure, unwilling to compromise or yield. When someone digs their heels in, they demonstrate a strong sense of determination and a refusal to back down. This can be both a strength and a weakness, depending on the situation. While it can be admirable to stand firm in one's beliefs, it is also important to be open to new ideas and willing to compromise.

Example: She dug her heels in and refused to accept the unfair terms of the deal.

Doggy Bag

Meaning: A container for taking leftover food home from a restaurant.

Origin: This playful phrase paints a picture of a restaurant patron discreetly requesting a container for their leftover meal. The term "doggy bag" suggests a lighthearted excuse to take home leftovers, implying the food is intended for a furry friend. The origin of the phrase is somewhat unclear, but it is believed to have emerged in the mid-20th century. It's possible the term was initially used to disguise the true purpose of taking home leftovers, as it was once considered somewhat impolite. By suggesting the food was for a pet, diners could avoid any social stigma.

Example: I couldn't finish my pasta, so I asked for a doggy bag to take it home.

Don't Have a Leg to Stand On

Meaning: To have no valid argument or support for one's position.

Origin: "Don't have a leg to stand on" is a vivid phrase from British English in the late 16th century. It likely refers to chairs and stools, where each time a leg is removed, the person sitting on it has less support. The phrase is often used in legal contexts to describe a case that lacks evidence or credibility. It can also be used in everyday conversations to indicate that someone's position is weak or indefensible.

Example: Without proof of purchase, you don't have a leg to stand on in demanding a refund.

Don't Put All Your Eggs in One Basket

Meaning: To avoid risking everything on a single opportunity or plan.

Origin: A timeless proverb commonly attributed to Miguel de Cervantes, who wrote *Don Quixote* in 1605. The quote from the book is, "It is the part of a wise man to keep himself today for tomorrow, and not venture all his eggs in one basket." This idiom encourages diversification and risk management. It suggests that it's wise to spread one's resources and efforts across multiple opportunities, reducing the potential for devastating loss.

Example: When investing, it's wise not to put all your eggs in one basket.

Double Cross

Meaning: To betray or deceive someone who trusted you.

Origin: The term "double-cross" originally referred to cheating in sports gambling when a contestant would break their word after promising to lose. Today, it means to deliberately betray someone or violate a promise or obligation. This idiom continues to describe any situation where someone is betrayed or deceived. It serves as a warning about the dangers of trusting the wrong people and the importance of being cautious in one's dealings with others.

Example: He promised to help but double-crossed us at the last moment.

Down and Out

Meaning: To be destitute or in a state of extreme poverty or misfortune.

Origin: The phrase "down and out" is an Americanism that originated in the 1880s or 1890s. The earliest known use of the phrase was in 1894 in the Daily Picayune of New Orleans. The phrase evokes a sense of hopelessness and despair, highlighting the challenges faced by those who have fallen on hard times. It serves as a reminder of the fragility of human existence and the importance of empathy and compassion.

Example: After losing his job, he felt completely down and out.

Down the Hatch

Meaning: A toast or encouragement to drink something, often alcohol.

Origin: During the 16th century, a sailor realized the correlation between a ship's hatch and a person's mouth and came up with the phrase. Over the years, it evolved as a metaphor for the act of swallowing a drink, with the throat being likened to the ship's hatch through which the liquid passes "down" into the stomach. The phrase suggests a quick and efficient consumption of a beverage, often alcoholic. It's a common toast or cheer, encouraging others to drink up and enjoy themselves. The imagery of something being swallowed or consumed, like cargo being loaded into a ship, highlights the satisfying nature of a good drink.

Example: Here's to your health—down the hatch!

Drag One's Feet

Meaning: To delay or act reluctantly in completing a task.

Origin: "Drag one's feet" is a vivid phrase that paints a picture of reluctance and delay. It conjures the image of someone walking slowly, deliberately dragging their feet along the ground. This physical action is a metaphor for a lack of enthusiasm or a deliberate attempt to avoid a task. The phrase is often used to describe someone who is procrastinating or avoiding a responsibility. It suggests a lack of motivation or a desire to delay. By "dragging their feet," a person is essentially stalling and avoiding taking action.

Example: Stop dragging your feet and finish your homework.

Draw a Blank

Meaning: To fail to recall or find an answer.

Origin: The idiom "draw a blank" originated in Tudor England during the reign of Queen Elizabeth I. It comes from the practice of national lotteries, where participants' names were put in one pot and notes with prizes or blanks were put in another. When names and prizes were drawn simultaneously, sometimes a name would be paired with a blank note, leading to the term "drawing a blank." When someone draws a blank, they are unable to remember a fact, solve a problem, or come up with a creative idea. It's a common experience that can be frustrating, especially during a test, a job interview, or a conversation. The phrase is a reminder that even the sharpest minds can sometimes experience lapses in memory or creativity.

Example: I tried to remember his name but completely drew a blank.

Dressed to the Nines

Meaning: To be dressed elegantly or fashionably.

Origin: A phrase that evokes the image of someone impeccably dressed, adorned in their finest attire. It conjures the picture of a person who has put considerable effort into their appearance, paying attention to every detail of their outfit. The exact origin of the phrase is somewhat mysterious, but it's believed to have Scottish roots. One theory suggests that it may be an application of the idiom "to the nines," which means "to perfection" or "to the highest degree."

Example: She arrived at the gala dressed to the nines in a stunning gown.

Drive Someone Up the Wall

Meaning: To annoy or irritate someone greatly.

Origin: A vivid phrase that paints a picture of intense irritation and annoyance. It conjures the image of someone climbing a wall, a desperate attempt to escape a frustrating or infuriating situation. This metaphor highlights the escalating levels of frustration and annoyance that can be caused by certain people or circumstances. The phrase is often used to describe someone particularly irritating or a situation that is especially stressful or frustrating. It suggests a high level of annoyance or agitation, as if the person is being driven to the point of madness.

Example: His constant humming is driving me up the wall.

Drum Up

Meaning: To generate interest, support, or business.

Origin: A vivid phrase that paints a picture of active solicitation and promotion. It conjures the image of a drummer beating their instrument to gather a crowd or announce an event. This metaphor highlights the energetic and proactive nature of drumming up interest or support. The phrase is commonly used in business and marketing contexts to describe the process of generating excitement and enthusiasm for a product, service, or event. It can also be used in a more general sense to mean encouraging or persuading people to participate in something. By "drumming up" interest, businesses and organizations can attract customers, raise awareness, and ultimately achieve their goals.

Example: The team worked hard to drum up support for their new product.

E

Early Bird

Meaning: Someone who arrives or acts before others, often to gain an advantage.

Origin: This proverb first appeared in William Camden's 1605 book of proverbs. The idea is that birds that wake up early have the best chance of catching a meal because other birds haven't woken up yet. The proverb means that people who are well-prepared are usually the most successful. This idiom is commonly used to describe someone who is an early riser or someone quick to act or seize an opportunity. It emphasizes the value of punctuality, diligence, and initiative. By being an early bird, one can gain a competitive edge and increase their chances of success.

Example: "Maria is always the early bird, arriving at the office before anyone else and getting a head start on her work."

Eat Humble Pie

Meaning: To admit a mistake or apologize for something wrong.

Origin: The phrase "eat humble pie" originated in the 1830s as a play on words. At the time, the "h" in "humble" was often dropped in pronunciation, so the phrase was changed to "humble pie." The word "umble" is no longer used in the language, but the phrase remains. To "eat humble pie" is to acknowledge one's mistakes, apologize, and accept responsibility. It's a metaphorical act of swallowing one's pride and accepting a lower social status, even if temporarily. This phrase is often used to describe situations where someone has to admit they were wrong or apologize for their behavior.

Example: After losing the argument, he had to eat humble pie and apologize to his colleague.

Egg on One's Face

Meaning: To look foolish or be embarrassed, usually after making a mistake.

Origin: The origin of this phrase is uncertain, but it is believed to have emerged from vaudeville and slapstick comedy routines, where performers were sometimes pelted with eggs as a form of audience disapproval. This physical act of humiliation has been transformed into a metaphorical expression that captures the feeling of public shame and embarrassment. When someone has "egg on their face," they have made a mistake that has been exposed to public scrutiny. This can be a humiliating experience, as it can damage one's reputation and credibility.

Example: He walked into the meeting with egg on his face after forgetting the presentation details.

Enter the Lion's Den

Meaning: To enter a situation where one is likely to face hostility or danger.

Origin: The phrase "enter the lion's den" comes from the story of Daniel in the lions' den in the Book of Daniel in the Bible. In the story, Daniel was thrown into a lions' den for praying to God against the king's orders. God sent an angel to protect Daniel, and he was unharmed the next day. When someone "enters the lion's den," they are voluntarily placing themselves in a difficult or confrontational situation. It could be a tense meeting with a hostile boss, a debate with a strong opponent, or simply facing a challenging task. The phrase highlights the courage and bravery required to confront adversity head-on.

Example: Going into that negotiation felt like entering the lion's den with all the tough competition.

Every Rose Has Its Thorns

Meaning: Every good thing comes with some challenges or difficulties.

Origin: The proverb "Every rose has its thorn" originated as a French or Italian saying. It is similar to the Persian saying, "He who wants a rose, must respect the thorn." This metaphor highlights the bittersweet nature of life, suggesting that even the most positive experiences or people come with challenges or drawbacks. It's a reminder to appreciate the good things in life while also acknowledging their imperfections.

Example: Starting a new business is exciting, but remember, every rose has its thorns.

Eye of a Needle

Meaning: A very small or narrow opening, often representing something difficult to achieve.

Origin: The phrase may refer to a small gate in Jerusalem that opened after the main gate closed at night. The gate was so small that a camel would need to be stooped over and have its baggage removed to pass through. The phrase is used in the Bible in the context of Jesus saying it is difficult or impossible for a rich man to enter heaven. The analogy is that a rich man would need to unload his material possessions to enter heaven, similar to how a camel would need to unload its baggage to pass through the gate. The phrase often describes a situation that is extremely difficult or unlikely to occur. It emphasizes the challenges faced by someone trying to achieve a particular goal or overcome an obstacle. The biblical reference to a camel passing through the eye of a needle further reinforces the idea of something that is virtually impossible.

Example: It's a challenge to get all the documents in on time—like trying to fit a camel through the eye of a needle!

F

Facing a Strong Headwind

Meaning: To face a difficult or challenging situation.

Origin: The phrase "facing a strong headwind" originates from nautical and aviation contexts. A headwind is a wind blowing directly opposite to the direction in which a ship or airplane is traveling, creating resistance and making it harder for the vessel to move forward, requiring more effort to maintain progress. In everyday language, the phrase has evolved to describe situations where one encounters significant challenges or obstacles that impede progress. Just as a strong headwind makes it tougher for a plane or ship to advance, facing a strong headwind metaphorically means dealing with difficult circumstances or opposition.

Example: We're facing a strong headwind with the new regulations, but we'll find a way to adapt.

Fall from Grace

Meaning: To lose status, respect, or favor, often due to a mistake or wrongdoing.

Origin: The term evokes the image of a sudden and dramatic decline in status or reputation, drawing inspiration from the Bible, specifically the King James Version of the Apostle Paul's letter to the Galatian church. In the letter, Paul warns that those justified by the law have fallen from grace. This metaphor highlights the idea of a loss of favor or privilege, often due to a moral lapse or significant mistake. When someone "falls from grace," they experience a significant decline in their social, professional, or personal standing. This can be due to various reasons, such as a scandal, public misstep, or moral failing. The phrase emphasizes the fragility of reputation and the consequences of poor choices.

Example: After the scandal, he experienced a dramatic fall from grace in the public eye.

Fall into Place

Meaning: To become clear or orderly after a period of confusion or difficulty.

Origin: This phrase evokes the image of a puzzle coming together, piece by piece. It suggests a sense of order and clarity emerging from chaos. This metaphor highlights the idea that, with time and effort, seemingly complex problems can be resolved. When something "falls into place," it means that the situation becomes clear, understandable, or manageable. It suggests that the various elements of a problem or situation are aligning, leading to a resolution or solution. This phrase is often used to describe a positive outcome, a happy ending, or a sense of relief after a period of difficulty.

Example: Once we got the funding, everything started to fall into place for the new project.

Fall through the Cracks

Meaning: To be overlooked or neglected, often unintentionally.

Origin: When something "falls through the cracks," it means that it has been neglected or forgotten. It can refer to a task that has been overlooked, a person who has been ignored, or a problem that has gone unnoticed. This phrase highlights the importance of attention to detail and the potential consequences of overlooking important matters. By understanding the origins and nuances of this phrase, we can better appreciate its power to convey the idea of neglect and the importance of ensuring that nothing falls through the cracks.

Example: The email must have fallen through the cracks; I didn't get a response until today.

Fast Track Something

Meaning: To expedite the completion of a project or task.

Origin: The term "fast track" originated in the English language as a compound of the words "fast" and "track." The earliest known use of the term was in the 1850s, and the first recorded use was in 1859 in the *Daily Sun* of Columbus, Georgia. This dynamic phrase, born from the world of railroad transportation, has become synonymous with expedited action. It evokes the image of a project moving with unprecedented speed and efficiency, bypassing the usual delays and obstacles. Whether it's a critical software launch, a crucial research endeavor, or a long-awaited construction project, "fast tracking" implies a commitment to swift execution and a determination to achieve results with unprecedented speed.

Example: We need to fast track this project to meet the new deadline.

Feeding Frenzy

Meaning: A situation where people or groups are eagerly competing for something, often with intense and chaotic energy.

Origin: The term "feeding frenzy" originated in the mid-20th century to describe a shark attack. The idea of a feeding frenzy was popularized in the 1958 book *Shark Attack* by V.M. Coppleson. In the modern world, a "feeding frenzy" can describe anything from a sudden rush on a hot new product to a frenzied media scrum surrounding a celebrity scandal. It captures the chaotic energy, the intense competition, and the often ruthless pursuit of a desired goal, whether it be fame, fortune, or simply a piece of the action.

Example: The media went into a feeding frenzy when the celebrity scandal broke.

Feeling Groggy

Meaning: To feel sluggish or disoriented, usually from lack of sleep or after an illness.

Origin: The word "groggy" comes from the noun "grog," which was a drink of rum diluted with water that was popular with sailors in the 1700s. The word "groggy" originally meant to be under the influence of grog, feeling tipsy, weak, or dazed. Today, the term "groggy" is used more broadly to describe a feeling of drowsiness, disorientation, or sluggishness, often experienced after waking up from sleep, recovering from an illness, or consuming alcohol. It evokes a sense of mental and physical fogginess, a difficulty in focusing or coordinating one's thoughts and movements. The term "groggy" effectively captures the feeling of being out of sorts, as if one is still partially submerged in a hazy, dreamlike state.

Example: I'm feeling groggy after that long flight, but a coffee should help.

Feeling Under the Weather

Meaning: To feel ill or unwell.

Origin: Imagine a stormy sea, the ship tossed about by raging waves. Below deck, amidst the swaying timbers and the creaking of the hull, lie the sickened sailors, sheltered from the tempestuous weather above. This is the origin of the evocative phrase "feeling under the weather." In the 19th century, when sailors fell ill, they were often confined to the depths of the ship, away from the fresh air and the ever-shifting currents of the sea. This metaphorical "below deck" became synonymous with a state of unwellness, a feeling of being out of sorts, as if one were experiencing the metaphorical equivalent of seasickness. Today, when we say we're "feeling under the weather," we evoke that same sense of being adrift, of experiencing a mild indisposition that keeps us from fully engaging with the world around us. It's a gentle reminder of the fragility of our health and the importance of finding respite when we need it.

Example: I'm feeling a bit under the weather today, so I think I'll stay home.

Fifty-Fifty

Meaning: To divide something equally, with a 50% chance or share for each side.

Origin: "Fifty-fifty" perfectly captures the essence of equal division. It evokes the image of a perfectly balanced scale, with two sides weighing exactly the same amount. This simple yet profound phrase has its roots in dividing something into two equal halves. Whether it's splitting a bill at a restaurant, sharing chores, or dividing a prize pool, "fifty-fifty" ensures fairness and equality. The phrase is deeply ingrained in our everyday language, a testament to the human desire for fairness and equity. It's a simple yet powerful concept, reminding us of the importance of sharing and cooperation.

Example: We'll split the cost of dinner fifty-fifty.

Fight Tooth and Nail

Meaning: To fight with great effort, persistence, and determination.

Origin: The idiom "fight tooth and nail" comes from the Middle English phrase "(with) nayles and teþ," which means "viciously, ferociously." It literally translates to "(with) nails and teeth." This phrase emphasizes the intensity and tenacity with which one fights to achieve a goal or protect something important.

Example: She fought tooth and nail to keep her company from going bankrupt.

Find Your Feet

Meaning: To become comfortable or confident in a new situation.

Origin: The idiom "find your feet" originated in the early 1600s and is thought to come from the act of finding balance or footing, especially when learning to walk or navigating uneven ground. Over time, the phrase came to have a more figurative meaning, referring to gaining confidence and stability in various aspects of life. When we "find our feet" in a new job, a new relationship, or a new environment, we are essentially gaining confidence, learning the ropes, and becoming comfortable in our surroundings. We are discovering our balance, our footing, and navigating our way through the unfamiliar.

Example: After a few weeks on the job, I finally feel like I've found my feet.

Fit as a Fiddle

Meaning: To be in excellent health or condition.

Origin: The phrase "fit as a fiddle" dates back to the 1600s in British English, but it meant something slightly different back then. The word "fit" had nothing to do with health but meant "well-suited" or "built for a particular purpose," the way we would say "fit for a purpose." Over time, the word "fit" came to mean "in good physical shape," and the phrase came to mean "in good condition physically."

Example: After my morning jog, I'm feeling as fit as a fiddle.

Fits the Bill

Meaning: To be exactly what is needed or required.

Origin: The phrase "fits the bill" has theatrical origins that go back to the early 19th century. The bill in question refers to a playbill, the list of dramatic pieces or parts that an actor was expected to perform. If an actor was deemed suitable for a specific role, they were said to fit the bill.

Example: This candidate fits the bill for the role perfectly.

Fly the Nest

Meaning: To leave home, especially when children become independent.

Origin: This evocative phrase draws a direct parallel between the natural world and human development. Just as a young bird spreads its wings and leaves the protective confines of the nest to explore the world, so too do human children eventually leave home to pursue their own lives. The phrase "fly the nest" symbolizes the transition to independence, the process of leaving the familiar comforts of the parental home and venturing out into the world. It's a bittersweet moment, filled with both pride and a touch of sadness, as parents watch their children spread their wings and embark on their own journeys.

Example: After college, she decided it was time to fly the nest and move to the city.

Flying High

Meaning: To be very successful or in a state of great happiness.

Origin: The expression "flying high" originated in the mid-1600s and is used to describe a high state of feeling or elation. It suggests a state of euphoria, a sense of accomplishment, and a feeling of being on top of the world. Whether it's achieving a personal goal, experiencing a romantic success, or simply enjoying a moment of pure joy, "flying high" perfectly describes that feeling of exhilaration and effortless grace.

Example: After closing the biggest deal of his career, he was flying high.

Fool's Gold

Meaning: Something that appears valuable but is actually worthless.

Origin: Fool's gold refers to pyrite, a mineral that resembles gold but has little worth. Miners in the 19th century often mistook it for real gold. Imagine a gold prospector, his heart pounding, unearthing a shimmering nugget. With excitement, he pockets the find, only to discover later, to his dismay, that it's not gold at all, but pyrite, a mineral that superficially resembles gold but lacks its value. This tragicomic scenario perfectly encapsulates the essence of "fool's gold." The phrase has extended beyond the realm of geology, now used to describe any situation where something initially appears valuable or promising but ultimately proves to be disappointing or worthless. It serves as a cautionary tale, reminding us to look beyond superficial appearances and to carefully examine the true value of opportunities and pursuits.

Example: That investment seemed promising, but it turned out to be fool's gold.

Fools Rush In

Meaning: People who act impulsively without thinking things through.

Origin: This timeless saying, penned by the renowned poet Alexander Pope in his 1711 masterpiece *An Essay on Criticism*, offers a profound observation on human behavior. It paints a vivid picture of the reckless and impulsive nature of some individuals, who, driven by folly or a lack of foresight, plunge headlong into situations that even the most cautious and discerning would avoid. Imagine a novice hiker, oblivious to the dangers, venturing into treacherous terrain that even experienced mountaineers would approach with trepidation. This is the essence of "fools rushing in," a stark reminder that caution and prudence are often the wiser course of action.

Example: Despite having no experience in the field, he hastily invested all his savings into the startup. As they say, fools rush in!

Fresh as a Daisy

Meaning: To feel rejuvenated or full of energy.

Origin: The idiom "fresh as a daisy" originated in the 19th century and comes from the Old English phrase "daes eage," which means "day's eye." The phrase refers to the way daisies open and close based on the amount of sunlight they receive. Whether it's after a good night's sleep, a refreshing swim, or a rejuvenating vacation, the phrase "fresh as a daisy" perfectly describes that feeling of renewed vigor and vitality. It's a compliment that suggests a sense of freshness, liveliness, and youthful exuberance.

Example: After a good night's sleep, I felt as fresh as a daisy in the morning.

Fun and Games Until Someone Loses an Eye

Meaning: A situation that starts as harmless fun but can quickly turn serious or dangerous.

Origin: The idiom "It's all fun and games until someone loses an eye" originated in Ancient Rome, where the only rule in wrestling was that eye gouging was not allowed. This historical context highlights the shift from what starts as a seemingly harmless and enjoyable activity to one with serious, sometimes grave, consequences. The phrase serves as a cautionary reminder that even activities meant for entertainment can have significant risks if not approached with caution.

Example: The kids were having a blast playing with their new slingshots, but I had to remind them that it's all fun and games until someone loses an eye.

G

Game Plan

Meaning: A strategy or plan for achieving a goal.

Origin: This term originates from sports, particularly football, where a "game plan" is devised to determine how to win the game. Just as a football coach meticulously plans each play to outmaneuver the opponent, so too do individuals and organizations develop "game plans" to achieve their objectives. This term, born from the world of sports, has become a ubiquitous part of our everyday vocabulary. Whether it's planning a business venture, preparing for an exam, or navigating a personal challenge, having a "game plan" is crucial for success. It provides a roadmap, a sense of direction, and a framework for making informed decisions. The image of a skilled coach orchestrating a winning strategy perfectly encapsulates the importance of careful planning and execution.

Example: Before the big meeting, let's make sure we have a solid game plan.

Get a Kick Out of Something

Meaning: To enjoy or find something amusing.

Origin: The term comes from sports, where a "kick" refers to the excitement or thrill of scoring a goal. Just as a soccer player experiences a thrill and a sense of accomplishment after scoring a goal, so too do we "get a kick out of" something that brings us joy or amusement. The image of a player celebrating a goal, feeling the adrenaline surge, perfectly captures the essence of this phrase – a sense of exhilaration, a moment of triumph, and a feeling of pure enjoyment.

Example: I really get a kick out of watching stand-up comedy on weekends.

Get a Life

Meaning: To stop focusing on trivial things and start living more fully.

Origin: This phrase became popular in the 1980s, often used in a sarcastic or critical way. It suggests that someone is spending too much time on insignificant pursuits and needs to start engaging in meaningful activities. This idiom often targets individuals who seem overly obsessed with trivial matters, such as celebrity gossip, social media, or niche interests. It implies that these individuals are wasting their time and energy on meaningless pursuits, neglecting more fulfilling aspects of life – building meaningful relationships, pursuing personal passions, and engaging with the world around them. Essentially, "get a life" is a call to action, a nudge towards a more fulfilling existence. It encourages individuals to step outside their comfort zones, explore new interests, and embrace a richer, more meaningful life experience.

Example: Instead of obsessing over social media, maybe you should get a life and enjoy real-world experiences.

Get Cold Feet

Meaning: To become nervous or hesitant, especially before a big decision or event.

Origin: The phrase first appeared in an 1878 English translation of the German novel *Seed-time and Harvest,* when a character leaves the poker table when his luck—and his feet, allegedly—are cold. When someone "gets cold feet," they experience a sudden surge of doubt or fear, often in the face of a challenging or unfamiliar situation. This can manifest in various ways, from a reluctance to speak in public to a sudden fear of commitment. The phrase is a reminder that even the most confident individuals can experience moments of doubt and apprehension. It highlights the importance of recognizing and managing these feelings, whether it's taking a deep breath, seeking support, or simply acknowledging the fear and proceeding with caution.

Example: She was excited about the trip, but when the time came to leave, she got cold feet.

Get Down to Business

Meaning: To stop wasting time and start focusing on important tasks.

Origin: This phrase is a direct and concise idiom that perfectly captures the essence of focusing on the task at hand. It evokes the image of a team or an individual shifting their attention away from distractions and frivolous pursuits to concentrate on the serious work that needs to be done. The phrase is often used in professional settings to encourage productivity and efficiency. It's a call to action, a reminder to prioritize tasks, eliminate distractions, and achieve desired outcomes. Whether it's a board meeting, a team brainstorming session, or simply an individual tackling a challenging project, the phrase "get down to business" serves as a powerful reminder to focus on the task at hand and achieve the desired results.

Example: Let's get down to business and finalize the budget proposal.

Get Off One's High Horse

Meaning: To stop acting arrogantly or superior to others.

Origin: The idiom "get off one's high horse" originated from the practice of medieval soldiers and landowners riding large horses to display their power and superiority over their subjects. The phrase "on one's high horse" dates back to the late 1700s and means to behave in an arrogant or condescending manner. For example, "When they started talking about music, David got on his high horse and said that classical music was only fit for museums and archives." The phrase "get off one's high horse" is a call for humility and empathy. It's a reminder that everyone is equal, regardless of their social status or perceived importance. By "getting off their high horse," individuals can cultivate more respectful and meaningful relationships with others.

Example: Stop being so condescending and get off your high horse!

Get Off Scot-Free

Meaning: To escape without punishment or consequences.

Origin: The idiom "get off scot-free" comes from the Old English word "scotfrēo," which means "exempt from royal tax or imposts." "Scot" was a tax levied on members of a village or town in medieval England, and the amount paid was based on the size of the person's property or land. People who avoided paying the tax were said to be "scot-free." Today, the phrase is used more broadly to describe any situation where someone avoids punishment or negative consequences. It can refer to escaping blame for a mistake, avoiding a fine, or even getting away with a crime. The phrase serves as a reminder that sometimes, luck plays a role, and individuals can escape situations that should have resulted in negative consequences.

Example: He was caught cheating but got off scot-free with just a warning.

Get on a Soapbox

Meaning: To speak passionately about a subject, especially in a public or unsolicited manner.

Origin: The phrase has its roots in a very literal sense. In the 19th and early 20th centuries, street corner orators would often use wooden crates used to transport soap as makeshift platforms to deliver their speeches. These "soapboxes" provided a raised platform, making the speaker more visible and their voice more audible to the passing crowd. This imagery of someone standing on a raised platform, passionately delivering their opinions to an unsuspecting audience, perfectly captures the essence of "getting on a soapbox." It implies a tendency to lecture or preach, often without being invited or solicited. Today, the phrase is used to describe anyone who expresses their opinions forcefully and at length, often in a way that may be perceived as preachy or overly enthusiastic.

Example: Whenever he gets on his soapbox about climate change, no one can interrupt him.

Get Out of Dodge

Meaning: To leave quickly, usually to avoid trouble or danger.

Origin: This evocative phrase draws its origins from the Wild West, specifically Dodge City, Kansas, a notorious frontier town known for its lawlessness and gunfights. Dodge City, with its saloons, gambling halls, and frequent showdowns, became synonymous with danger and chaos. The phrase "get out of Dodge" conjures the image of a weary traveler, perhaps a cowboy or a stagecoach driver, sensing trouble brewing and making a hasty exit from the town before things turn violent. It implies a quick and decisive departure, a need to escape a potentially dangerous or uncomfortable situation as quickly as possible. Today, the phrase is used more broadly to describe any situation where it's advisable to leave quickly, whether it's a social gathering that's gone sour, a heated argument, or simply a desire to escape from a mundane or unpleasant environment.

Example: After the argument, it was clear we needed to get out of Dodge before things escalated.

Get Someone's Goat

Meaning: To irritate or annoy someone.

Origin: This evocative phrase originates from the world of horse racing. In the early days of racing, goats were often placed in the stalls with the horses to keep them calm. If a rival stable hand removed the goat, the horse would become agitated and perform poorly, giving the rival an unfair advantage. This act of deliberate sabotage, designed to upset and frustrate the horse, is the very essence of "getting someone's goat." It implies a deliberate attempt to annoy or irritate someone, to throw them off their game, and to hinder their success. Today, the phrase is used more broadly to describe any situation where someone is intentionally provoked or irritated. It can refer to petty annoyances, deliberate sabotage, or any action designed to disrupt someone's peace of mind.

Example: His constant humming really gets my goat!

Get the Lead Out

Meaning: To hurry up or get moving faster.

Origin: The phrase likely originates from the world of transportation, specifically the use of lead weights to balance objects. Imagine a wagon or cart laden with heavy lead weights, struggling to move. To improve its speed, the driver would need to "get the lead out" – remove the heavy weights that were slowing it down. This concept of removing a heavy burden to increase speed has evolved into a common idiom. It's a forceful instruction to hurry up, to increase one's pace, and to eliminate any factors that are hindering progress. Whether it's a deadline looming, a task that's dragging on, or a general sense of sluggishness, "get the lead out" is a powerful reminder to accelerate and move forward with greater speed and efficiency.

Example: We need to get the lead out if we want to make it to the meeting on time!

Get Under One's Skin

Meaning: To annoy or irritate someone.

Origin: The phrase likely originates from the feeling of discomfort or irritation that arises when something gets physically under your skin. Just as an insect crawling under your skin causes an incessant itch, so too can certain people or situations cause a similar level of annoyance and frustration. The phrase evokes the image of something that is deeply irritating, something that burrows beneath the surface and causes a constant sense of unease. It might be a persistent noise, a nagging habit, or a personality trait that constantly rubs you the wrong way. This vivid metaphor perfectly captures the feeling of being constantly bothered, of having something or someone persistently chipping away at your patience and composure.

Example: His constant complaining really gets under my skin.

Get Wind of

Meaning: To hear about or learn of something, often by accident.

Origin: The idiom "get wind of" originated during the era when sailing was the primary method of long-distance travel. The wind could carry the scent of land, other ships, or even food cooking on board, allowing sailors to be alerted to something before they could see it. The expression alludes to an animal perceiving a scent carried by the wind. The phrase emphasizes the unexpected nature of the information, suggesting that it has reached us through indirect means, perhaps through a network of whispers and rumors.

Example: I got wind of their secret plans during lunch today.

Getting Hitched

Meaning: To get married.

Origin: The idiom "getting hitched" is thought to have originated in the 1840s. It's an informal phrase that means to get married, and is a metaphor for a couple coming together in marriage, similar to horses being hitched to a wagon. The horses share the responsibility of pulling the load, just as a couple shares responsibility in a marriage. The phrase "getting hitched" is a lighthearted and informal way to describe the act of marriage. It emphasizes the idea of two individuals being "bound" together, forming a partnership and embarking on a new chapter in their lives.

Example: They're getting hitched next weekend, and I can't wait to attend the wedding!

Give a Leg Up

Meaning: To help someone advance or improve, especially in a difficult situation.

Origin: The idiom "give someone a leg up" originated in the first half of the 1800s and is a reference to helping someone get on a horse by placing their foot in the stirrup. Just as one might offer a helping hand to someone trying to mount a horse, "giving a leg up" in a metaphorical sense means offering assistance to someone who is struggling or facing a challenge. This phrase implies a willingness to help, to offer support and encouragement to someone who needs it. It can refer to offering practical assistance, such as providing guidance or resources, or simply offering words of encouragement and support. The image of someone lending a helping hand, literally or metaphorically, perfectly encapsulates the spirit of this phrase – a willingness to assist others and to help them succeed.

Example: The mentorship program really gave me a leg up in my career.

Glass Ceiling

Meaning: An invisible barrier that prevents people, especially women, from advancing in their careers or achieving higher positions.

Origin: Coined in the 1970s by Marilyn Loden, an American author and diversity advocate, the term "glass ceiling" refers to the unseen, yet very real, obstacles that prevent groups from advancing to top positions within organizations. Imagine a ceiling made of glass – transparent, yet impenetrable. You can see the positions of power above, but you're unable to reach them. This powerful imagery perfectly illustrates the invisible barriers that women and minorities often encounter in their careers, such as unconscious bias, discrimination, and lack of mentorship. The "glass ceiling" highlights the systemic inequalities that persist in many workplaces, despite progress towards greater diversity and inclusion.

Example: She's been in the same position for years because of the glass ceiling in her company.

Gnash One's Teeth

Meaning: To show frustration, anger, or pain, often in a symbolic way.

Origin: The phrase has its roots in the Bible, where it is often used to describe the lamentation of the damned in hell. The image of teeth grinding together in agony and despair is a powerful metaphor for intense suffering and frustration. Today, the phrase is used more broadly to describe any situation where someone is experiencing intense anger, frustration, or resentment. It can be used to describe someone who is feeling helpless, powerless, or deeply disappointed.

Example: He gnashes his teeth every time he loses a game.

Go the Extra Mile

Meaning: To put in more effort than what is expected or required.

Origin: This idiom comes from the Bible, specifically the Gospel of Matthew, where Jesus says, "If anyone forces you to go one mile, go with him two." This biblical passage emphasizes the importance of going above and beyond what is expected, of extending kindness and generosity even when it's not strictly required. It encourages us to be selfless, to put forth extra effort, and to treat others with compassion and understanding. Today, "go the extra mile" has become a common idiom used to encourage individuals to exceed expectations, strive for excellence, and demonstrate a commitment to going above and beyond in their work, relationships, and all aspects of life.

Example: She always goes the extra mile to make sure every project is perfect.

Go the Whole Nine Yards

Meaning: To do something to its fullest extent or complete it entirely.

Origin: The most widely accepted origin of the phrase lies in World War II aviation. Fighter planes of that era carried ammunition belts that were nine yards long. Pilots who "gave 'em the whole nine yards" were firing all their ammunition, going all-out in the fight. This image of a pilot unleashing a barrage of firepower, using every last bullet, perfectly encapsulates the meaning of "going the whole nine yards." It implies exerting maximum effort, giving one's all, and leaving nothing in reserve. Today, the phrase is used in various contexts to describe any situation where someone gives their absolute best, whether it's completing a challenging task, putting on a spectacular performance, or simply enjoying a meal to the fullest.

Example: When planning the party, they went the whole nine yards with decorations and entertainment.

Good Samaritan

Meaning: A person who helps others selflessly, often in a time of need.

Origin: The parable of the Good Samaritan, found in the Gospel of Luke, tells the story of a traveler who is robbed and beaten, left for dead on the side of the road. While priests and Levites pass him by, a Samaritan, a member of a group traditionally viewed with hostility by the Jews, stops to help. He tends to the injured man's wounds, provides him with shelter and care, and even pays for his lodging. This powerful parable emphasizes the importance of compassion, kindness, and selfless service towards others, regardless of social or religious differences. The "Good Samaritan" has become a symbol of altruism, a reminder that we have a moral obligation to help those in need, even if it means going out of our way to do so. The term "Good Samaritan" now refers to anyone who acts compassionately and selflessly to help others, often at personal cost. It is a powerful reminder of the importance of human kindness and the profound impact that acts of compassion can have on the world.

Example: The stranger who helped me fix my flat tire was a true Good Samaritan.

Goody Two-Shoes

Meaning: A person who is virtuous to the point of being overly moral or self-righteous.

Origin: The term comes from a 1765 English children's story called "Goody Two-Shoes," about a poor, virtuous girl who only had one pair of shoes. Overjoyed to receive a second pair, she exclaims, "Two shoes! Two shoes!" This simple expression of gratitude, repeated throughout the story, became associated with excessive virtue and piety. The character of Goody Two-Shoes, with her unwavering goodness and seemingly endless supply of virtuous deeds, became a somewhat satirical figure. The phrase "Goody Two-Shoes" evolved to describe someone who is excessively virtuous, overly moralistic, and perhaps a bit smug about their own goodness. It often carries a hint of irony, suggesting that their constant striving for virtue may be insincere or even self-serving. The story of Little Goody Two-Shoes, though intended to be uplifting, ironically gave rise to a term that is often used with a touch of sarcasm or disapproval.

Example: She's always following the rules—such a goody two shoes!

Got It in the Bag

Meaning: To be certain of success or victory.

Origin: This idiom likely originated in the world of sports in early 20th century America with the New York Giants baseball team. The idiom comes from a superstition that the team developed during a 26-game winning streak in 1916. The Giants would put a bag of extra baseballs on the field at the start of each game. If the Giants were in the lead in the ninth inning, they would carry the bag off the field to ensure victory. The team believed that carrying the bag meant they had "captured the game in the bag." The phrase is used to express confidence and certainty in achieving a goal. It suggests that success is imminent, that victory is all but assured. Whether it's landing a job, winning a competition, or achieving any other desired outcome, "having it in the bag" implies a strong sense of optimism and a high degree of confidence in a successful outcome.

Example: With her experience, she's got it in the bag for the interview.

Graveyard Shift

Meaning: A work shift that takes place during the night, typically from midnight to the early morning.

Origin: The term likely comes from the eerie quietness of working late at night when only the sound of gravestones and the occasional nocturnal creature can be heard, creating a "graveyard" atmosphere. Imagine working in a factory or hospital during the dead of night, surrounded by an eerie silence, the only sounds being the ticking of a clock and the occasional distant howl. This image perfectly captures the essence of the "graveyard shift," a time when most of the world is asleep. The term itself conjures up images of stillness and solitude, of working in a near-ghostly environment. It's a shift often associated with a sense of isolation and a unique brand of quiet energy. While some may find the "graveyard shift" appealing, offering a sense of peace and tranquility, it undoubtedly presents its own set of challenges, requiring a unique blend of resilience and adaptability.

Example: I have to work the graveyard shift tonight, so I'll be sleeping all day tomorrow.

Gray Area

Meaning: A situation that is unclear or not easily categorized.

Origin: Just as the color gray lies between black and white, a "gray area" represents a situation that is not clearly defined or easily categorized. It's a space where boundaries are blurred, and it's difficult to determine what is right or wrong, acceptable or unacceptable. The metaphor of gray, with its subtle shades and nuances, perfectly illustrates the complexities of such situations. It highlights the difficulty of making clear distinctions and the challenges of navigating situations that fall outside of established norms or rules. In today's world, many ethical, social, and political issues exist within a "gray area," where there are no easy answers and multiple perspectives must be considered. The phrase "gray area" serves as a reminder that the world is not always black and white, and that navigating the complexities of life often requires us to think critically and make nuanced judgments.

Example: The new policy leaves a lot of gray areas that need further clarification.

Grin and Bear It

Meaning: To endure something unpleasant or difficult with a smile or good attitude.

Origin: The phrase "grin and bear it" originated from the Old English word grinnian, which means "to show one's teeth in pain or anger." "To bear" in this context means to endure. The phrase is used to describe accepting something unpleasant or difficult without complaining because there is no other option. Whether it's enduring a long and tedious task, tolerating a difficult person, or dealing with a disappointment, "grin and bear it" encourages us to face challenges with resilience and a positive attitude, even when we'd rather be doing something else.

Example: I didn't enjoy the long meeting, but I had to grin and bear it.

H

Happy as a Lark

Meaning: Very cheerful or carefree.

Origin: The phrase draws its imagery from the carefree and joyful nature of the lark, a small bird renowned for its melodious song and its seemingly effortless flight. Imagine a lark soaring through the sky, singing its cheerful tune, seemingly without a care in the world. This image of effortless joy and freedom perfectly mirrors the feeling of someone who is "happy as a lark." The phrase evokes a sense of pure, unadulterated happiness, a feeling of lightness and freedom from worry. It suggests a state of contentment and exuberance, a feeling of pure joy and delight.

Example: Ever since she found out she got the job, she's been happy as a lark, smiling all day.

Hard and Fast

Meaning: Strict or unchangeable.

Origin: The phrase "hard and fast" originated as a nautical term to describe a ship that was out of water, either because it was in dry dock or had run aground. The term was first recorded between 1865 and 1870, but it was used figuratively by the mid-1800s. Imagine a ship stranded on a sandbar, its hull firmly embedded in the sand. It's "hard and fast," unable to move, stuck in its position.

This image of something firmly fixed and immovable is the essence of the phrase "hard and fast." Today, we use "hard and fast" to describe rules, deadlines, or any other situation that is inflexible and allows for no exceptions. It implies a strict adherence to rules and regulations, with no room for deviation or compromise.

Example: The rules are hard and fast—there's no room for exceptions.

Hard Nut to Crack

Meaning: A difficult problem or person to understand or deal with.

Origin: The phrase "hard nut to crack" originates from the literal act of trying to crack open a hard-shelled nut, metaphorically representing something difficult to solve or deal with. Essentially, the "nut" is a challenging problem, and "cracking" it means finding a solution, with the "hardness" indicating the level of difficulty involved. It suggests that a significant amount of effort and determination will be required to achieve success.

Example: Getting him to agree to the proposal was a hard nut to crack.

Have One Foot in the Grave

Meaning: To be close to death or in very poor health.

Origin: The phrase "have one foot in the grave" means someone is very close to death or very old, and its origin can be traced back to 17th century English literature, with the earliest recorded use appearing in the play *The Fatal Dowry* by Philip Massinger and Nathan Field, where the line "When one foot's in the graue" is found. At that time, "foot" could also be used as a verb meaning "to trip" or "catch," so the phrase would have implied being trapped by death with no escape. This graphic metaphor highlights the fragility of human life and the inevitability of death. It's a poignant reminder of our mortality and the limited time we have on this earth. While the phrase may seem morbid, it can also serve as a powerful motivator, encouraging us to make the most of our time and live life to the fullest.

Example: Despite feeling like he had one foot in the grave, he still managed to come to work today.

Have One's Heart Set on Something

Meaning: To strongly desire or be determined to achieve something.

Origin: The phrase beautifully uses the "heart" as a metaphor for deep-seated emotions and aspirations. When you "have your heart set on something," your deepest desires and passions are fully invested in achieving that particular goal. Imagine a child intently focused on building the perfect sandcastle, their entire attention and energy directed towards their creation. This is the essence of "having one's heart set on something" – a deep-seated desire, a passionate focus, and an unwavering commitment to achieving a specific goal. This idiom emphasizes the power of strong desires and the importance of pursuing one's passions with dedication and perseverance.

Example: She has her heart set on getting into the university of her dreams.

Have Someone Over a Barrel

Meaning: To be in a situation where someone has no choice but to agree or comply.

Origin: It stems from the historical practice of reviving someone who had drowned. In the past, a common method of reviving a drowning person was by placing them face down over a barrel to drain water from their lungs. This position left the individual completely helpless and dependent on the actions of those attempting to revive them. This image of someone lying face down, completely at the mercy of others, perfectly captures the essence of the phrase. "Having someone over a barrel" implies a situation where one has no power or control, completely at the mercy of another's demands. The phrase evokes a sense of vulnerability and helplessness, highlighting the feeling of being completely reliant on the actions of another.

Example: He had me over a barrel, insisting I sign the contract on the spot.

Have the Last Laugh

Meaning: To ultimately succeed or triumph, especially after others doubted or mocked you.

Origin: The phrase comes from the idea of the final, victorious laugh after a situation has played out. It suggests that, despite earlier failures or ridicule, the person who "has the last laugh" ends up on top. Imagine a person who has been doubted and mocked for pursuing an ambitious dream. After years of hard work and perseverance, they finally achieve success, silencing their critics and enjoying the sweet satisfaction of proving them wrong. This is the essence of "having the last laugh." It's a phrase that celebrates resilience, perseverance, and the ultimate triumph of the human spirit. It's a reminder that setbacks are temporary, and that with dedication and determination, even the most challenging goals can be achieved.

Example: Everyone doubted her plan, but she had the last laugh when it was a success.

Have Your Cake and Eat It Too

Meaning: To enjoy two desirable but usually incompatible things at once.

Origin: The phrase "you can't have your cake and eat it too" originated as "a man can not have his cake and eat his cake" in a letter from Thomas, Duke of Norfolk, to Thomas Cromwell in 1538. The phrase means that you can't have two good things at the same time, especially if they are not usually possible to have together. The phrase is a reminder that life often involves making choices and accepting compromises. It serves as a caution against unrealistic expectations and the pursuit of mutually exclusive desires. While it may seem tempting to "have your cake and eat it too," the reality is that we often have to make choices and accept the consequences of those choices.

Example: You can't have your cake and eat it too—either focus on your career or take a long vacation.

Head off at the Pass

Meaning: To prevent something before it happens.

Origin: This vivid phrase originates from the American West, conjuring images of cowboys and outlaws in the Wild West. In the days of cattle drives and stagecoach robberies, a narrow mountain pass was a strategic point of control. By "heading off" someone at the pass, you could intercept them before they could reach their destination or carry out their plans. This image of anticipating and preventing action, of blocking someone's path before they can proceed, perfectly captures the essence of the phrase. Today, "head off at the pass" is used more broadly to describe any situation where you anticipate a problem and take steps to prevent it from occurring. Whether it's addressing a potential conflict, preventing a mistake, or anticipating a challenge, "heading off at the pass" emphasizes the importance of proactive action and the ability to anticipate and prevent problems before they arise.

Example: We need to head this problem off at the pass before it gets out of hand.

Head on a Platter

Meaning: To offer someone up for punishment, often in a figurative sense.

Origin: The phrase comes from ancient times when beheadings were a form of punishment. It directly references the biblical story of the beheading of John the Baptist, where, according to the Gospels, his head was presented to King Herod Antipas on a platter after he was executed at the request of Herodias, his wife's daughter Salome. This essentially signified a readily offered sacrifice or a situation where someone is easily defeated or handed over to their enemy. The phrase "head on a platter" is used metaphorically to describe a situation where someone is facing severe consequences, often as a result of their actions or the actions of others. It implies a sense of impending doom, a situation where the stakes are incredibly high, and the consequences could be dire. The image of a severed head, presented on a platter as a macabre offering, serves as a potent reminder of the serious consequences that can arise from certain actions.

Example: After the company's major blunder, the CEO's head was on a platter, figuratively speaking.

Heads Up

Meaning: A warning or advance notice about something.

Origin: The phrase originated from military usage, where it meant for soldiers to literally hold their heads high, signifying alertness, courage, and vigilance in tough situations—essentially telling them to "keep their chin up." This usage dates back to the late 18th century. Over time, it evolved to become a general warning phrase, indicating that someone should be aware of something coming their way or a potential danger ahead. It can be a simple warning about an incoming object, a friendly reminder about an upcoming event, or a heads-up about a potential problem. "Heads up!" is a concise and effective way to communicate a quick warning or alert, encouraging others to be prepared and attentive.

Example: Just a heads up—there's a meeting scheduled for 3 PM today.

Heart Is in the Right Place

Meaning: To have good intentions, even if the results aren't perfect.

Origin: This phrase refers to the idea that the heart is the seat of emotions, so when someone's heart is "in the right place," it means they are motivated by good, kind feelings, even if their actions or results aren't flawless. Just as a compass guides a traveler towards their destination, a person with their "heart in the right place" is guided by a genuine desire to do good, to help others, or to make a positive impact. Their intentions may be pure, even if their actions sometimes fall short of the mark. This idiom emphasizes the importance of judging people not solely by their actions, but also by their underlying motivations. It acknowledges that while mistakes are inevitable, the intention behind our actions often reveals the true character of our hearts.

Example: Even though the project didn't go as planned, her heart was in the right place.

Hedge Your Bets

Meaning: To take precautions by not putting all your resources or hopes into one outcome.

Origin: The phrase "hedge your bets" originates from the word "hedge," which originally referred to a physical barrier or fence used to protect crops in agriculture, signifying the idea of creating a protective boundary. The phrase itself first appeared in a play in 1672, where it described the act of minimizing losses on a bet by taking out smaller loans from different lenders, essentially "hedging" against potential risk by diversifying options. When we "hedge our bets" in everyday life, we are essentially taking steps to minimize potential losses and increase our chances of success. This might involve pursuing multiple career paths, exploring different options, or making backup plans.

Example: It's smart to hedge your bets by applying to multiple job openings instead of just one.

Hell Bent

Meaning: Determined to do something at all costs, often recklessly.

Origin: The phrase "hell bent" means extremely determined or recklessly intent on something, and its origin comes from combining the word "hell" (representing a strong, forceful intent) with "bent" which means inclined or determined, essentially signifying a level of determination so strong that it's like being "bent on going to hell" to achieve a goal. The earliest known usage dates back to the mid-1700s. Think of a runaway train, hurtling down the tracks, unable to stop, destined for a collision. This image perfectly captures the essence of "hell bent," a state of reckless determination that can be both exhilarating and terrifying.

Example: He's hell bent on making this project work, no matter what.

Hit the Hay

Meaning: To go to bed or sleep.

Origin: In the past, hay was commonly used as a mattress filler, providing a simple and rustic bed for weary souls. The image of "hitting the hay" – literally lying down on a bed of hay – perfectly captures the act of going to sleep, of seeking rest and rejuvenation after a long day's work. It's a simple yet evocative phrase that has endured for generations, a testament to the enduring human need for rest and relaxation.

Example: It's late—I'm going to hit the hay and get some rest.

Hold on for Dear Life

Meaning: To hang on tightly, often in a dangerous or risky situation.

Origin: The phrase "hold on for dear life" means to cling to something with all your strength, usually in a dangerous situation, and while the exact origin isn't clear, it likely dates back to the 18th century where "for dear life" simply meant "with all your might" or "as if your life depended on it." This image of desperate clinging, of holding on with all one's might, perfectly captures the essence of the phrase. It evokes a sense of urgency and fear, a situation where the stakes are high and the consequences of letting go are dire. Whether it's facing a personal crisis, overcoming a challenging obstacle, or simply navigating a chaotic situation, "holding on for dear life" implies a determined effort to maintain control, persevere through adversity, and emerge from the storm unscathed.

Example: She held on for dear life as the rollercoaster plunged down the tracks.

Hold One's Tongue

Meaning: To keep quiet or refrain from speaking.

Origin: This idiom originates from the medieval practice of using a tongue-in-cheek gesture, symbolizing silence. The phrase emphasizes the physical act of restraining speech. It evokes the image of literally holding one's tongue, preventing oneself from speaking. This could be a conscious effort to remain silent, to avoid saying something hurtful or inappropriate, or to simply refrain from interrupting. The image of physically restraining one's tongue perfectly captures the essence of the phrase—the act of consciously suppressing the urge to speak, of choosing silence over words.

Whether it's to avoid a conflict, to maintain composure, or to show respect for others, "holding one's tongue" is a valuable skill that requires self-control and a conscious effort to restrain one's impulses.

Example: I had to hold my tongue during the meeting, even though I disagreed with their approach.

Hold the Fort

Meaning: To take care of things in someone's absence.

Origin: During the American Civil War, Union General William Tecumseh Sherman famously sent a message to a besieged garrison at Allatoona Pass in Georgia: "Hold the fort for I am coming!" This message, delivered by telegraph, became a rallying cry for the defenders, urging them to hold their ground against the Confederate attack. The image of soldiers bravely defending a fort against enemy assault perfectly captures the essence of "holding the fort." It implies a responsibility to maintain a position, defend a territory, and ensure that everything remains secure in the absence of the commander. Today, the phrase is used more broadly to describe any situation where someone is asked to take charge and maintain order in the absence of another. Whether it's watching children while a parent runs errands, managing a project while a colleague is away, or simply keeping things running smoothly during a temporary absence, "holding the fort" implies a responsibility to maintain stability and ensure that everything continues to function smoothly.

Example: Can you hold the fort while I run some errands?

Hold Your Horses

Meaning: To wait or slow down.

Origin: In Book 23 of the *Iliad*, Homer writes "Hold your horses!" when referring to Antilochus driving like a maniac in a chariot race that Achilles initiates in the funeral games for Patroclus. This image of controlling a powerful force, of restraining one's impulses, has evolved to encompass a broader range of situations. Today, we use "hold your horses" as a way to urge someone to slow down, to be patient, and to think before they act. It's a reminder to exercise caution, to avoid rushing into things, and to consider the potential consequences before proceeding.

Example: Hold your horses! We need to make sure everything is ready before we start.

Hook, Line, and Sinker

Meaning: To completely believe or fall for something, often without question.

Origin: This vivid phrase draws its imagery directly from the world of fishing. When a fish "swallows the hook, line, and sinker," it has completely fallen for the angler's deception, ingesting not just the bait, but also the hook, line, and the weight attached to it. This image of complete and utter deception perfectly captures the essence of the idiom. It implies a situation where someone has been completely fooled, believing in something without question or reservation. Whether it's a convincing scam, a persuasive sales pitch, or simply a compelling story, "falling for something hook, line, and sinker" implies a complete and utter gullibility, a lack of skepticism, and a willingness to believe something without any critical examination.

Example: He believed their story hook, line, and sinker, and ended up losing a lot of money.

I

If the Creek Don't Rise

Meaning: A phrase used to say that something will happen as long as nothing unexpected occurs.

Origin: While in the South, Benjamin Hawkins, an Indian agent in the late 1700s and early 1800s, was requested by the President of the U.S. to return to Washington. In his response, he was said to write, "God willing and the Creek don't rise." Because he capitalized the word "Creek," it is deduced that he was referring to the Creek Indian tribe and not a body of water. This nuanced interpretation adds a layer of historical and cultural significance to the phrase, highlighting the specific context and the potential challenges associated with his work among the Native American populations of the South.

Example: I'll see you at the party tomorrow, if the creek don't rise.

In a Pickle

Meaning: In a difficult or troublesome situation.

Origin: The phrase originates from the 17th-century process of pickling, where food is preserved in a brine solution. While pickling preserves food, the process itself can be somewhat unpleasant. Imagine a cucumber submerged in a vat of vinegar, trapped and unable to escape. This image of being confined and preserved, often in a somewhat unpleasant state, perfectly captures the essence of "being in a pickle." It describes a situation where someone feels trapped, constrained, or in a difficult predicament. They may feel stuck, unable to find a way out, and perhaps even a bit overwhelmed by the challenges they face.

Example: I found myself in a pickle when I realized I had double-booked my appointments.

In Broad Daylight

Meaning: During the daytime, in full view, often referring to something done openly or without trying to hide.

Origin: The phrase "in broad daylight" originates from the literal meaning of "daylight," signifying that something happens openly and visibly during the day when people can easily see what is occurring. "Broad" here emphasizes the full extent of daylight, making the visibility even more apparent. The phrase emphasizes the audacity and brazenness of an action, suggesting that it was done openly, without any attempt at secrecy or discretion.

Example: The thief stole the car in broad daylight, right in front of everyone!

In Deep Waters

Meaning: In a difficult, complicated, or dangerous situation.

Origin: This idiom originates from the idea of being in deep water where one can't stand and might easily drown. Imagine a swimmer unexpectedly finding themselves far from shore, struggling to stay afloat in deep water. The waves crash around them, the current pulling them further and further from safety. This image of being out of one's depth, struggling to maintain control, perfectly encapsulates the meaning of "in deep water." The phrase evokes a sense of vulnerability and danger, a feeling of being overwhelmed and out of control. It suggests a situation where one is facing significant challenges, where the stakes are high, and where the outcome is uncertain. Whether it's a complex personal problem, a difficult professional challenge, or a financial crisis, "being in deep water" implies a situation that requires significant effort, ingenuity, and perhaps a bit of luck to navigate successfully.

Example: After missing several deadlines, he found himself in deep water with his boss and had to work overtime to make amends.

In for a Penny, In for a Pound

Meaning: If you are going to get involved in something, you might as well go all the way.

Origin: This phrase comes from old British currency, where a penny and a pound were seen as vastly different in value. The idiom suggests that if you've invested a small amount (a penny), you might as well commit to a larger amount (a pound) if the situation calls for it. Imagine an entrepreneur investing a small amount of seed capital in a new business venture. If the initial investment shows promise, the idiom "in for a penny, in for a pound" encourages them to fully embrace the opportunity, perhaps by investing more capital, dedicating more time, and taking greater risks to achieve success. This phrase serves as a reminder that sometimes, the greatest rewards come from taking calculated risks and committing fully to a chosen course of action.

Example: We've already spent a lot of time on this project—so in for a penny, in for a pound!

In High Spirits

Meaning: Feeling very cheerful or happy.

Origin: The phrase comes from the idea of being "spirited," with "spirits" referring to emotions or feelings. The phrase evokes the image of someone filled with energy and enthusiasm, their mood elevated and buoyant. Just as a hot air balloon ascends high into the sky, their spirits are lifted, soaring above any negativity or gloom. The concept of "spirits" itself refers to the emotions and feelings that animate a person. When someone is "in high spirits," their emotions are elevated, their mood is cheerful, and they are filled with a sense of joy and optimism.

Example: She was in high spirits after receiving the good news about the promotion.

In One's Neck of the Woods

Meaning: In one's local area or region.

Origin: This evocative phrase originates from rural America, where "neck of the woods" originally referred to a specific area within a larger forested region. It conjures images of a small community nestled within a larger wilderness, a familiar and intimate territory where everyone knows everyone else. The phrase emphasizes a sense of belonging and familiarity. It suggests a deep connection to one's local environment, a comfort with the people, places, and customs of one's own community. Today, "in one's neck of the woods" has evolved to encompass any local area, whether it's a rural community, a bustling city neighborhood, or even a specific social or professional circle. It's a phrase that evokes a sense of belonging, of being at home and comfortable within one's own familiar territory.

Example: I'm from a small town in the Midwest—if you're ever in my neck of the woods, let me know!

In Seventh Heaven

Meaning: In a state of extreme happiness or bliss.

Origin: This evocative phrase draws its origins from ancient and medieval cosmology, where the concept of multiple heavens existed. In these belief systems, the universe was often envisioned as a series of concentric spheres or layers, with each successive level ascending towards a higher state of existence. The seventh heaven, being the highest and most exalted of these celestial spheres, was considered the abode of God, angels, and the blessed. It was a place of ultimate bliss, a paradise where all desires were fulfilled. This concept of the seventh heaven as the pinnacle of happiness has been carried into modern language. When someone is "in seventh heaven," they are experiencing a state of pure ecstasy, a feeling of overwhelming joy and contentment.

Example: When he got engaged, he was in seventh heaven.

In the Black/Red

Meaning:

- **In the Black:** Financially in a good position, making a profit.
- **In the Red:** Financially in a bad position, operating at a loss.

Origin: Imagine an accountant reviewing a company's financial records. Profits are typically recorded in black ink, while losses are often recorded in red ink. This visual distinction between black and red has become a powerful metaphor for financial health.

- **In the Black:** This signifies a state of financial prosperity, where income exceeds expenses. It evokes a sense of stability, success, and a positive financial outlook.
- **In the Red:** Conversely, being "in the red" implies financial difficulty, where expenses exceed income, resulting in debt or financial instability.

These two contrasting phrases, born from the world of accounting, have entered common parlance to describe not only financial situations but also broader aspects of life. For example, someone might be "in the red" emotionally after a difficult breakup, or "in the black" in terms of their overall well-being after achieving a personal goal. The contrast between these two colors, black and red, serves as a powerful metaphor for the spectrum of financial and emotional states, from prosperity and success to difficulty and struggle.

Example: After a successful quarter, the company is finally in the black again.

In the Dark

Meaning: Uninformed or unaware about something.

Origin: The phrase "in the dark" originates from the idea that darkness represents a lack of knowledge or ignorance, meaning when someone is "in the dark" about something, they are unaware or uninformed about it. This metaphor dates back to the late 1600s and is used to describe a situation where someone is intentionally or unintentionally kept from knowing information. The phrase "in the dark" highlights the importance of transparency and open communication. It serves as a reminder that withholding information can have detrimental consequences, creating misunderstandings, fostering distrust, and hindering progress.

Example: I was completely in the dark about the surprise party until I walked in.

Isn't Over Till the Fat Lady Sings

Meaning: It's not finished or decided until the very end.

Origin: This idiom originates from the world of opera, specifically referencing the powerful and dramatic arias often sung by soprano soloists at the climax of a performance. These powerful vocal performances often signify the culmination of the opera, the final act before the curtain falls. This idiom is frequently used in sports commentary, political races, and any other situation where the outcome is uncertain. It encourages a cautious optimism, reminding us that even when victory seems assured, unforeseen circumstances can still arise.

Example: Don't give up hope just yet—remember, it isn't over till the fat lady sings!

It's All Greek to Me

Meaning: Something that is unintelligible or difficult to understand.

Origin: This idiom has its roots in the Middle Ages, when Latin was the dominant language of scholarship and religion. During this time, Greek was often seen as a complex and esoteric language, understood only by scholars and intellectuals. Imagine a medieval monk encountering a manuscript written in Greek. To him, the text would be utterly unintelligible, a series of meaningless symbols. This image of facing something completely incomprehensible, something beyond one's understanding, perfectly captures the essence of "it's all Greek to me." The phrase has evolved to describe any situation where something is completely baffling or confusing. It's used to express bewilderment, frustration, and a complete lack of understanding. The metaphor of Greek, a language perceived as foreign and mysterious, effectively conveys the feeling of being completely lost, of encountering something that is utterly beyond one's comprehension.

Example: I tried reading the technical manual, but it was all Greek to me.

J

Jekyll and Hyde

Meaning: A person who has two very different sides to their personality, often one being kind and the other being cruel or violent.

Origin: The phrase originates from Robert Louis Stevenson's chilling novella, *The Strange Case of Dr. Jekyll and Mr. Hyde*. In this gothic tale, Dr. Jekyll, a respected and benevolent scientist, unwittingly unleashes his darker side, Mr. Hyde, a monstrous and evil persona. This chilling story, with its exploration of the darker aspects of human nature, has left an indelible mark on our language. The phrase "Jekyll and Hyde" now serves as a potent metaphor for anyone who exhibits sudden and dramatic shifts in personality, behavior, or mood. Whether it's someone who is charming and sociable one moment and irritable and aggressive the next, or a company that shifts abruptly from ethical practices to ruthless exploitation, the term "Jekyll and Hyde" perfectly captures the unsettling duality of human nature.

Example: He's such a Jekyll and Hyde—one minute he's friendly, the next he's angry and distant.

Jump for Joy

Meaning: To be extremely happy or excited about something.

Origin: This idiom is a direct reflection of our natural human tendency to physically express our emotions. When we experience intense joy or excitement, our bodies often respond with spontaneous movements, such as jumping, clapping, or dancing. Imagine a child receiving a long-awaited gift, their excitement so palpable that they leap for joy, their arms raised in triumph. This image perfectly captures the essence of the phrase. "Jump for joy" is a vivid and universally understood expression that transcends cultural boundaries. It's a simple yet powerful way to describe a state of pure elation, a feeling so intense that it compels us to express it physically.

Example: She jumped for joy when she found out she got the job!

Jump to Conclusions

Meaning: To make a judgment or decision without having all the facts.

Origin: The image of someone leaping forward without looking, without considering the potential obstacles or pitfalls, perfectly mirrors the act of making a hasty decision. When we "jump to conclusions," we are essentially making assumptions, drawing inferences, and forming opinions without fully understanding the situation. This can lead to misinterpretations, misunderstandings, and potentially harmful consequences. The phrase serves as a cautionary reminder to gather all the relevant facts, consider all perspectives, and carefully weigh the evidence before forming an opinion or making a decision. By avoiding the temptation to "jump to conclusions," we can make more informed and considered judgments, leading to better outcomes in our personal and professional lives.

Example: Don't jump to conclusions about the project before hearing all the details from the team.

K

Keep a Stiff Upper Lip

Meaning: To remain calm and composed, especially in difficult or stressful situations.

Origin: "Keep a stiff upper lip" is deeply rooted in British culture, particularly the Victorian era, where emotional restraint and stoicism were highly valued. Imagine a Victorian gentleman facing adversity, perhaps a personal loss or a financial setback. Instead of openly expressing his grief or despair, he would "keep a stiff upper lip," maintaining a composed and dignified demeanor, despite the turmoil within. This image of emotional restraint, of suppressing one's emotions in the face of adversity, perfectly captures the essence of the phrase. It reflects a cultural ideal of stoicism and resilience, where displaying one's emotions openly was considered a sign of weakness. While the emphasis on emotional restraint may seem outdated in today's society, the underlying message of courage and resilience in the face of adversity remains relevant. "Keeping a stiff upper lip" encourages us to maintain our composure, to face challenges with dignity, and to persevere through difficult times with grace and fortitude.

Example: Even when the news was disappointing, he kept a stiff upper lip and didn't show his frustration.

Keep One's Head Above Water

Meaning: To manage to survive or continue in a difficult situation, especially financially or professionally.

Origin: This phrase comes from the idea of staying afloat in water, where you struggle to keep your head above the surface to avoid drowning. The image of someone struggling to stay afloat in deep water, desperately trying to keep their head above the surface, vividly illustrates the challenges of navigating difficult times. This metaphor emphasizes the effort and resilience required to overcome adversity. It suggests a situation where one is facing significant challenges, perhaps financial difficulties, overwhelming responsibilities, or personal struggles. "Keeping one's head above water" implies a constant struggle for survival, a relentless effort to maintain stability and avoid being completely overwhelmed by the challenges at hand. It's a reminder of the importance of resilience, perseverance, and the ability to adapt and overcome obstacles in the face of adversity.

Example: After losing his job, he's just trying to keep his head above water until he finds another opportunity.

Keep One's Shirt On

Meaning: To remain calm or patient; not to get angry.

Origin: The phrase likely originated from the custom of removing one's shirt before engaging in a physical fight. This act, while not always universal, was a common practice in certain cultures to allow for greater freedom of movement and to avoid damaging one's clothing during a scuffle. The image of someone keeping their shirt on, refraining from removing it and therefore avoiding a physical altercation, perfectly captures the essence of the idiom. It implies a conscious effort to maintain self-control, to avoid escalating a situation, and to choose diplomacy over confrontation. Today, "keep your shirt on" is used more broadly to encourage calm and restraint in any situation where emotions are running high. It's a reminder to think before acting, to choose our words carefully, and to avoid unnecessary conflict.

Example: Keep your shirt on, we'll get to your issue in just a minute.

Keep Pace

Meaning: To maintain the same speed or progress as others.

Origin: This idiom originates from the world of athletics, specifically running races. In a footrace, "keeping pace" with the other runners means maintaining the same speed, staying abreast of the competition, and avoiding falling behind. This image of maintaining a steady pace, of moving forward at an equal rate with others, perfectly captures the essence of the idiom. Beyond the realm of sports, "keeping pace" is used to describe a wide range of situations where maintaining a consistent level of progress or performance is crucial. Whether it's keeping up with the demands of a fast-paced job, adapting to changing technologies, or maintaining a healthy lifestyle, "keeping pace" emphasizes the importance of consistent effort and continuous growth.

Example: The new software is so fast, it's hard to keep pace with its updates.

Keep Someone on Their Toes

Meaning: To make sure someone is alert and ready for anything.

Origin: This phrase comes from the idea of standing on your toes, which requires balance and awareness. This vivid image emphasizes the need for constant awareness and responsiveness. It suggests a situation where one must remain alert, adaptable, and ready to react quickly to changing circumstances. Whether it's a demanding boss, a competitive sport, or a challenging relationship, "keeping someone on their toes" requires them to stay sharp, think quickly, and be constantly prepared for the unexpected. It's a reminder that complacency can be dangerous, and that maintaining a state of alertness and readiness is crucial for navigating the complexities of life.

Example: The manager likes to keep the team on their toes by frequently changing priorities.

Keep Under One's Hat

Meaning: To keep something secret or confidential.

Origin: This phrase comes from the idea of hiding something under a hat to keep it concealed. The phrase evokes the image of concealing something beneath one's hat, a personal and intimate space where secrets can be safely hidden from prying eyes. Just as a magician might conceal a hidden object beneath their hat, the phrase suggests a deliberate effort to keep information private, to prevent it from being shared or revealed to others. Whether it's a surprise party, a business secret, or a personal confidence, "keeping something under your hat" implies a commitment to discretion and a respect for the confidentiality of the information. The image of a secret being carefully concealed beneath one's hat serves as a powerful reminder of the importance of discretion and the value of keeping certain information private.

Example: You have to keep this news under your hat until the official announcement.

Knee High to a Grasshopper

Meaning: Referring to when someone was very young.

Origin: The phrase "knee high to a grasshopper" means someone is very young, and it originated in the United States around 1850, replacing earlier versions of the idiom that used different small insects like a mosquito, bumblebee, or splinter, with "grasshopper" eventually becoming the standard comparison; essentially signifying someone is so small they are only as tall as a grasshopper would be at the knee. The phrase is often used fondly to reminisce about childhood, to evoke a sense of nostalgia for a time of innocence and carefree play. It's a reminder of how much we've grown, both physically and emotionally, since those early years. The image of a child, small and insignificant compared to the vastness of the world around them, perfectly captures the essence of this idiom, reminding us of the preciousness of childhood and the importance of cherishing those early memories.

Example: I remember her knee-high to a grasshopper, running around with her brother.

Knock It out of the Park

Meaning: To do something extremely well, to perform beyond expectations.

Origin: This vivid idiom originates from the world of baseball, specifically the thrilling feat of hitting a home run. A home run, where the batter hits the ball so far that it clears the outfield fence entirely, is a rare and spectacular achievement. The image of a powerful swing, the ball soaring through the air and landing far beyond the field, perfectly captures the essence of this idiom. It evokes a sense of triumph, of surpassing all expectations, and achieving a level of success that is truly outstanding. Today, "knock it out of the park" is used to describe any exceptional performance, whether it's a brilliant presentation, a groundbreaking piece of art, or simply a job well done. It's a powerful compliment that signifies a level of achievement that goes above and beyond expectations.

Example: She really knocked it out of the park with her presentation today.

Knock One's Socks Off

Meaning: To impress someone greatly or surprise them.

Origin: The phrase evokes the image of someone being so surprised or excited that they are literally knocked off balance, their socks flying off in the process. This exaggerated image emphasizes the sheer force of the impact, the suddenness and intensity of the experience. Whether it's a breathtaking performance, a stunning piece of art, or an unexpected act of kindness, "knocking someone's socks off" implies an experience that is truly extraordinary, something that leaves a lasting and unforgettable impression. It's a powerful compliment that suggests a level of awe and admiration that goes beyond mere appreciation.

Example: The movie's special effects really knocked my socks off!

Knowledge Is Power

Meaning: Understanding and information give one control or influence.

Origin: This powerful idea is often attributed to Sir Francis Bacon, a renowned English philosopher and statesman. Bacon, a champion of scientific inquiry and empirical knowledge, first expressed the idea in his 1597 work *Meditationes Sacrae* where he wrote "ipsa scientia potestas est" which translates to "knowledge itself is power" in Latin; essentially meaning that having knowledge gives you power to influence and achieve things. He argued that through knowledge, individuals gain a deeper understanding of the world around them, enabling them to make informed decisions, solve problems, and exert greater control over their own destinies. The phrase "knowledge is power" emphasizes the transformative potential of learning. It suggests that by acquiring knowledge, we gain a deeper understanding of ourselves, the world around us, and our place within it. This knowledge, in turn, empowers us to make informed choices, navigate the complexities of life, and shape our own destinies. The pursuit of knowledge, therefore, is not merely an intellectual exercise, but a quest for empowerment, a journey towards greater understanding, and a path towards a more fulfilling and meaningful life.

Example: You can win any argument if you're prepared—knowledge is power!

Knuckle Down

Meaning: To focus and put in serious effort, especially when starting to work hard on something.

Origin: This idiom likely originates from the game of marbles, where players would "knuckle down" by placing their knuckles on the ground to steady their aim before shooting their marble. This physical act of grounding oneself, of finding stability and focus, is the essence of the phrase. The image of a player carefully positioning their knuckles, preparing for a precise shot, perfectly mirrors the act of focusing intently on a task. It suggests a commitment to serious effort, a willingness to concentrate and apply oneself fully to the challenge at hand. Today, "knuckle down" is used to encourage someone to apply themselves diligently, to focus their attention, and to work hard towards a particular goal. It's a reminder that success often requires dedication, perseverance, and a willingness to put in the necessary effort.

Example: We need to knuckle down and finish this report before this weekend."

L

Land on One's Feet

Meaning: To recover from a difficult situation or to come out well despite challenges.

Origin: This idiom draws its inspiration from the remarkable ability of cats to always land on their feet when falling. This natural instinct, this uncanny ability to right themselves and land safely, has become a powerful metaphor for human resilience. When someone "lands on their feet," they have successfully navigated a difficult situation, emerging unscathed and often even more successful than before. They have demonstrated remarkable adaptability, resourcefulness, and the ability to bounce back from setbacks. This phrase emphasizes the importance of resilience, the ability to overcome challenges and emerge stronger from adversity. It's a reminder that even in the face of setbacks, it's possible to find a way to succeed, to "land on one's feet" and continue moving forward.

Example: After the company downsized, she landed on her feet with a better opportunity at a competitor.

Lead Someone by the Nose

Meaning: To control or manipulate someone completely.

Origin: The phrase originates from the practice of leading animals, particularly livestock, by a ring or rope through their noses. This method of control, while necessary for managing animals, also highlights the vulnerability of the animal, completely at the mercy of its handler. This image of an animal being easily manipulated, with no control over its own direction, perfectly captures the essence of the idiom. When someone is "led by the nose," they are easily influenced, manipulated, or controlled by another person. They lack the autonomy and critical thinking skills to make their own decisions, blindly following the direction of another. The phrase emphasizes the importance of independent thought and the dangers of allowing oneself to be unduly influenced or manipulated by others.

Example: He always tries to lead his team by the nose, making all the decisions without consulting anyone.

Leaps and Bounds

Meaning: To make rapid or significant progress.

Origin: This vivid idiom originates from the world of nature, specifically the powerful and graceful movements of animals. Imagine a deer leaping across a field, covering vast distances with incredible speed and agility. This image of swift and impressive movement, of covering ground quickly and effortlessly, is the very essence of "leaps and bounds." The phrase evokes a sense of rapid growth and development, of achieving significant milestones in a short period of time. Whether it's a child's rapid development, a company's explosive growth, or an individual's personal transformation, "leaps and bounds" emphasizes the speed and magnitude of the progress. It's a powerful metaphor that highlights the potential for rapid advancement and encourages us to strive for continuous improvement and strive to achieve our goals with speed and agility.

Example: Her skills in the new software have improved in leaps and bounds since the training.

Leave Someone to Their Own Devices

Meaning: To allow someone to do something on their own, without assistance or interference.

Origin: The phrase originates from the concept of "devices," which in older usage referred to one's own plans, schemes, or methods. To "leave someone to their own devices" meant to allow them to pursue their own course of action, to handle a situation according to their own judgment and initiative. Imagine a child being left to entertain themselves, free to explore their own interests and devise their own games. This is the essence of "leaving someone to their own devices" – granting them autonomy, allowing them to think independently, and encouraging them to discover their own solutions. This phrase emphasizes the importance of independence and self-reliance. It suggests that by allowing individuals the freedom to act on their own, we empower them to learn, grow, and develop their own unique skills and abilities.

Example: The team was left to their own devices to finish the project on time.

Lend a Hand

Meaning: To offer help or assistance.

Origin: The phrase is rooted in the simple, yet profound, act of physically helping someone by extending a hand. Whether it's assisting someone with a heavy load, helping a neighbor in need, or offering support to a friend in distress, "lending a hand" emphasizes the importance of human connection and the value of helping others. This simple act of extending a hand, a gesture of physical and emotional support, has become a powerful symbol of kindness, compassion, and the importance of community. It reminds us that even small acts of assistance can make a significant difference in the lives of others.

Example: I'll lend a hand with the presentation if you need it.

Let Someone Have It

Meaning: To criticize, scold, or confront someone forcefully.

Origin: The phrase evokes the image of unleashing one's anger or frustration, of delivering a strong and forceful response to someone's words or actions. It suggests a verbal outburst, a forceful expression of displeasure, and a clear message that their behavior is unacceptable. Whether it's a scathing rebuke, a sharp criticism, or simply a forceful expression of disapproval, "letting someone have it" implies a strong and decisive response, a clear message that their behavior will not be tolerated. The phrase emphasizes the importance of asserting oneself and expressing one's displeasure when necessary, while also serving as a reminder of the importance of choosing one's words carefully and responding constructively.

Example: He let me have it for missing the meeting without any notice.

Let the Cat Out of the Bag

Meaning: To reveal a secret or disclose something that was supposed to be kept confidential.

Origin: This vivid idiom originates from a clever (and somewhat deceitful) practice used by some unscrupulous merchants in medieval times. They would sell piglets, conveniently packaged in sacks for easy transport. However, to increase their profits, some merchants would substitute a cat for the piglet within the sack. Imagine the buyer's surprise upon reaching home and "letting the cat out of the bag," only to discover they had been cheated. This image of an unexpected and unwelcome revelation perfectly captures the essence of the phrase. Today, "letting the cat out of the bag" refers to any situation where a secret is accidentally revealed, often causing embarrassment or disappointment. It serves as a reminder of the importance of discretion and the potential consequences of accidentally divulging confidential information.

Example: She accidentally let the cat out of the bag about the surprise party.

Life in the Fast Lane

Meaning: A lifestyle characterized by excitement, risk, or constant activity.

Origin: This evocative phrase draws its imagery directly from the world of driving. On a multi-lane highway, the "fast lane" is reserved for vehicles traveling at higher speeds. It's where the action is, where the thrill of speed and the excitement of the open road are most keenly felt. This image of high-speed travel, of pushing boundaries and embracing exhilaration, has extended beyond the literal realm of driving to describe a lifestyle characterized by excitement, adventure, and often, a degree of risk. "Living life in the fast lane" can refer to a career in a high-pressure field, a social life filled with constant activity and excitement, or simply a personal philosophy that embraces adventure and the thrill of the unknown. The phrase evokes a sense of dynamism, of constantly moving forward, of embracing challenges and pushing one's limits. It's a lifestyle that promises excitement and adventure, but also carries a degree of risk and uncertainty.

Example: After the promotion, he's living life in the fast lane, balancing work and adventure.

Life Is a Bowl of Cherries

Meaning: Life is pleasant, carefree, or full of enjoyable moments.

Origin: This cheerful idiom has its roots in a popular 1931 song of the same name, "Life Is Just a Bowl of Cherries," written by Lew Brown and Ray Henderson. The song, with its upbeat tempo and optimistic lyrics, quickly gained popularity, and the phrase itself became a common expression of optimism and contentment. Cherries, with their vibrant color, sweet taste, and association with summer, have long been a symbol of joy and abundance. The image of a bowl overflowing with luscious, ripe cherries evokes a sense of pleasure, indulgence, and effortless enjoyment. "Life is a bowl of cherries" suggests a carefree and optimistic outlook on life, a belief that happiness is readily available and that life is full of pleasant experiences. While life certainly has its challenges, the phrase encourages us to appreciate the good things, to savor the sweet moments, and to approach life with a positive and optimistic attitude.

Example: Ever since they got married, their life has been a bowl of cherries.

Lighten Up

Meaning: To become less serious, more relaxed, or to stop being overly critical.

Origin: Just as the weight of a heavy burden can be lessened, so too can the weight of stress and anxiety be alleviated. The phrase evokes the image of releasing tension, shedding worries, and embracing a more carefree and optimistic outlook. It's a gentle reminder to relax, to take things less seriously, and to find joy in the lighter side of life. Whether it's a reminder to take a break from a demanding task, to approach a situation with a more relaxed attitude, or simply to enjoy the present moment, "lighten up" encourages us to find joy and ease in our daily lives.

Example: You need to lighten up! It's just a minor mistake, not the end of the world.

Lightning Never Strikes Twice

Meaning: Misfortune or rare events are unlikely to happen in the same way again.

Origin: The phrase originates from the observation that lightning, a powerful and unpredictable force of nature, rarely strikes the same exact spot twice. This observation, while not entirely accurate in reality, became a metaphor for the improbability of experiencing the same rare or unfortunate event repeatedly. Whether it's a stroke of good luck, a devastating tragedy, or any other unusual occurrence, the phrase "lightning never strikes twice" suggests that such events are rare and unlikely to be repeated. While not scientifically accurate, the idiom effectively conveys a sense of caution and a reminder that while unfortunate events can happen, it's unlikely that the exact same circumstances will repeat themselves.

Example: After surviving that car accident, she believed that lightning never strikes twice, and she felt safe driving again.

Like a Broken Record

Meaning: To repeat the same thing over and over, often annoyingly.

Origin: The phrase originates from the era of vinyl records. When a record became scratched or damaged, the needle would often get stuck in a groove, causing the same section of music to play repeatedly. This frustrating experience of hearing the same phrase or melody over and over again is the very essence of the idiom. Today, "like a broken record" is used to describe anyone who repeats themselves excessively, often in a way that is annoying or tiresome to others. It serves as a gentle reminder to vary one's speech, to consider the perspectives of others, and to avoid repeating oneself unnecessarily.

Example: He sounds like a broken record when he keeps reminding me about the same issue.

Like Death Warmed Over

Meaning: Looking very ill or extremely tired.

Origin: The phrase evokes the chilling image of something that has returned from the brink, something that barely escaped death and is now recovering, but still appears pale, weak, and barely alive. It's a graphic and unsettling metaphor that emphasizes the severity of the person's condition. They may not be literally on the verge of death, but they appear extremely unwell, drained of energy, and perhaps even a little ghostly. "Like death warmed over" is a powerful phrase that vividly conveys the image of someone who is severely ill, exhausted, or simply looking unwell to the point of being almost unrecognizable.

Example: After the long flight, she looked like death warmed over and just wanted to sleep.

Like Taking Candy from a Baby

Meaning: Something that is very easy to do, almost too easy.

Origin: The phrase evokes the image of a child, innocent and trusting, easily tempted by the allure of sweet treats. Taking candy from a baby is not only easy but also considered somewhat unfair, as a child lacks the understanding or the ability to resist. This image of effortless acquisition, of something being easily obtained without any resistance, perfectly captures the essence of the idiom. It's used to describe any situation where something is achieved with remarkable ease, often implying that the task was significantly easier than anticipated.

Example: Winning the competition was like taking candy from a baby; no one else even came close.

Like Water off a Duck's Back

Meaning: Something that has no lasting effect; criticism or negative comments that don't bother you.

Origin: This vivid idiom draws inspiration from the natural world. Ducks have a unique oily coating on their feathers that repels water, causing it to simply bead up and roll off their backs. This image of water effortlessly sliding off a duck's back perfectly mirrors the idea of something having no impact. Criticism, insults, or even difficult situations seem to simply "roll off" the person, leaving them unaffected. The phrase emphasizes a sense of resilience, indifference, and an ability to remain unaffected by negativity or criticism. It suggests that the person is emotionally detached, impervious to the words or actions of others. Whether it's a seasoned politician shrugging off criticism or a confident individual ignoring the whispers of doubt, "like water off a duck's back" perfectly captures the ability to remain unfazed and unaffected by external pressures.

Example: His rude remarks were like water off a duck's back to me—I didn't let them bother me.

Live and Let Live

Meaning: To tolerate others' behaviors and allow them to live as they choose, without interference.

Origin: The phrase was first recorded in 1622 in *The Ancient Law Merchant* by G. De Malynes. The book was about the lex mercatoria, a system of law developed by medieval merchants to regulate commerce. The phrase "live and let live" encourages a spirit of tolerance and understanding, a willingness to accept others for who they are, even if their choices or beliefs differ from our own. It promotes a harmonious coexistence, where individuals are free to pursue their own paths without fear of judgment or interference. This philosophy of tolerance and acceptance is crucial for creating a more peaceful and harmonious society, where individuals feel free to express themselves and pursue their own happiness without fear of persecution or discrimination.

Example: They have different beliefs, but they agree to live and let live.

Live on a Shoestring

Meaning: To live with very little money or on a tight budget.

Origin: The exact origin of the phrase is uncertain, but it's generally believed to have originated in the United States in the 1800s. The phrase alludes to the fragility of a thin, weak shoestring. Imagine someone living on a very tight budget, carefully budgeting every dollar, making do with secondhand items, and finding creative ways to save money. This is the essence of "living on a shoestring" – making the most of limited resources, finding joy in simple pleasures, and navigating life with resourcefulness and resilience. The phrase serves as a reminder that happiness and fulfillment are not solely dependent on material wealth. It encourages us to appreciate the value of frugality, to find joy in simple pleasures, and to live within our means.

Example: They had to live on a shoestring during their first year in the city, but they managed to get by.

Living on Borrowed Time

Meaning: Living in a situation where death or failure is inevitable, but still managing to survive.

Origin: The phrase "living on borrowed time" was first recorded between 1870 and 1875. It's an idiom that means to continue to live past the expected time of death, or to continue doing something for longer than expected. For example, "Since his cancer was diagnosed, he feels as if he's living on borrowed time." This powerful metaphor highlights the fragility of human life and the preciousness of each moment. It encourages us to cherish the time we have, to appreciate the beauty of life, and to make the most of every opportunity. "Living on borrowed time" is a poignant reminder of our mortality and the importance of living each day to the fullest.

Example: After the accident, he felt like he was living on borrowed time and decided to make the most of it.

Long Shot

Meaning: A very unlikely or improbable event.

Origin: This idiom has its roots in the world of marksmanship and gambling. In the context of shooting, a "long shot" refers to a shot taken at a very distant target, where the chances of hitting the mark are slim. The phrase "long shot" originated in the 1880s and has multiple origins:

Early Firearms: The phrase may have originated from the idea that early naval guns were only effective at close range and were unlikely to hit a target at a great distance.

Gambling: The phrase may have originated in gambling over horse races, where a long shot was a bet with a low chance of winning.

Other Improbable Circumstances: By the late 19th century, the phrase had expanded to mean anything that seemed unlikely, such as a wild guess. The phrase can be used by itself or in the negative form "not by a long shot." "Not by a long shot" means not at all, not even close, or not even a tiny chance. The phrase emphasizes the challenging nature of the undertaking, highlighting the low probability of success and the significant obstacles that must be overcome.

Example: Winning the lottery is a long shot, but it's fun to dream!

Look Daggers at

Meaning: To stare at someone with intense anger or hostility.

Origin: The idiom "look daggers at" is a metaphor that compares an angry expression to a dagger's thrust. It has been used in English since around 1600 and alludes to a look that is so fierce that it could injure the person being looked at. Imagine a duel, where two adversaries face off, their eyes locked in a fierce and menacing stare. This is the essence of "looking daggers at someone" – a chilling display of hostility, a silent threat conveyed through a single, penetrating gaze. The phrase emphasizes the power of non-verbal communication, highlighting how a single look can convey a wealth of emotions, from anger and resentment to contempt and disdain.

Example: She looked daggers at me when I accidentally spilled the drink on her shirt.

Look What the Cat Dragged In

Meaning: Someone or something that appears unexpectedly, usually in a disheveled or unpleasant state.

Origin: This vivid idiom originates from the observation of feline hunting behavior. Domestic cats, in their playful nature, often bring home "trophies" of their hunts – dead mice, birds, or even the occasional unfortunate lizard. These "presents," while a testament to the cat's hunting prowess, are often not welcome by their human companions. The image of a cat dragging in a muddy, disheveled creature, perhaps a dead bird or a struggling mouse, perfectly captures the essence of the phrase. It evokes a sense of surprise, often tinged with a bit of disgust, at the unexpected and sometimes unpleasant arrival. Today, "look what the cat dragged in" is used to describe the unexpected arrival of a person or thing, often in a less than ideal state. It can refer to an unexpected guest, an unwelcome surprise, or simply someone who appears disheveled, tired, or generally out of sorts.

Example: Well, look what the cat dragged in—it's been years since I've seen you!

Loose Cannon

Meaning: A person who is unpredictable and uncontrollable, often creating trouble.

Origin: This vivid idiom originates from the world of naval warfare. On a sailing ship, cannons were securely mounted on the deck. However, during a storm or battle, a cannon could become dislodged, rolling freely across the deck and causing chaos and potential injury to the crew. This image of an uncontrolled and potentially destructive force perfectly captures the essence of the phrase. Today, "loose cannon" is used to describe any person who is unpredictable, uncontrollable, and potentially disruptive. It refers to someone who is prone to outbursts, who acts without thinking, and whose actions can have unintended and often negative consequences. The phrase evokes a sense of danger and unpredictability, highlighting the potential for chaos and disruption caused by someone who is out of control.

Example: He's a loose cannon in meetings—always saying something controversial without thinking.

Loose Lips Sink Ships

Meaning: Careless talk or revealing secrets can cause harm or damage.

Origin: During World War II, the United States government launched a public awareness campaign to encourage citizens to be mindful of their words. The slogan "Loose lips sink ships" was a central part of this campaign, used on posters, in public service announcements, and even on matchbooks. The phrase emphasizes the potential consequences of sharing sensitive information. During wartime, careless talk could reveal valuable intelligence to the enemy, potentially endangering military operations and putting lives at risk. The image of a ship, vulnerable to attack, sinking due to the careless words of others, serves as a powerful reminder of the importance of discretion and the potential dangers of sharing sensitive information. While the wartime context of the phrase has changed, the underlying message remains relevant today. In an age of rapid communication and instant information sharing, the dangers of careless talk can still have significant consequences, both personally and professionally.

Example: Be careful about what you say; loose lips sink ships.

Lose Your Marbles

Meaning: To go crazy, become confused, or lose one's mental clarity.

Origin: The phrase "lose your marbles" is an idiom that means to lose one's mind or go crazy. It's thought to have originated from the game of marbles, which was popular in the United States during the 1930s. The phrase may have been influenced by the idea that losing your marbles in the game meant losing the game.

The alliteration in the words "mind" and "marbles" may have also contributed to the phrase's popularity. This image of losing something valuable, something that represents a sense of order and control, has evolved to symbolize a loss of mental clarity or composure. The phrase vividly captures the image of someone losing their grip on reality, their behavior becoming unpredictable and erratic, much like the scattered and lost marbles of a child.

Example: After the long hours of work, I felt like I was about to lose my marbles.

Lost in Thought

Meaning: Deeply absorbed in one's own thoughts, often oblivious to what's happening around them.

Origin: The phrase "lost in thought" was first recorded around 1681. It's an idiom that means to be so focused on your own thoughts that you're not paying attention to anything else. The words "lost" and "thought" are combined to describe the state of being engrossed by something or preoccupied with mental activity. This vivid image emphasizes the power of the human mind to wander, to drift away from the immediate surroundings and become absorbed in internal thoughts, memories, or fantasies. When someone is "lost in thought," they may appear distracted, absent-minded, and oblivious to their surroundings. They may be daydreaming, pondering a problem, or simply lost in contemplation. The phrase "lost in thought" highlights the human tendency to become absorbed in our own internal worlds, a reminder that while our minds can take us to incredible places, it's important to remain grounded in the present moment and aware of our surroundings.

Example: She was so lost in thought during the meeting that she didn't even notice the presentation was over.

Lower the Bar

Meaning: To reduce standards or expectations, often making something easier or more attainable.

Origin: This idiom originates from the world of athletics, specifically high jump competitions. In high jump, the bar is raised progressively higher as the competition progresses. However, if the bar is "lowered," it becomes easier for the athletes to clear, effectively reducing the level of difficulty. This image of lowering the bar to make something easier to achieve perfectly captures the essence of the idiom. Today, "lower the bar" is used to describe any situation where standards or expectations are reduced. It can refer to a decline in academic standards, a relaxation of rules, or a decrease in the level of difficulty or quality. The phrase often carries a negative connotation, suggesting that lowering standards can lead to mediocrity and a lack of motivation to strive for excellence.

Example: The company had to lower the bar for candidates after struggling to fill the position.

Lower Your Guard

Meaning: To relax one's vigilance or defenses, often leading to vulnerability.

Origin: This idiom originates from the world of fencing, where a "guard" refers to a defensive position, a posture that protects the fencer from attack. Lowering one's guard means dropping this defensive posture, leaving oneself open to attack. This image of lowering one's defenses, of becoming less vigilant and more susceptible to harm, perfectly captures the essence of the phrase. Beyond the literal world of fencing, "lowering your guard" is used to describe any situation where someone becomes less cautious, more trusting, or less vigilant. It can refer to sharing personal information with someone you don't fully trust, letting your emotions get the best of you, or simply relaxing your vigilance in a potentially risky situation. The phrase serves as a reminder of the importance of maintaining a healthy level of caution and awareness, of being mindful of potential threats, and of not letting our guard down unnecessarily.

Example: She finally lowered her guard and allowed herself to trust him completely.

M

Magic Bullet

Meaning: A simple solution to a complex problem, often perceived as a quick fix.

Origin: This phrase originates from the early 20th century, where the idea of a "magic bullet" was introduced in medicine, referring to a substance that could specifically target and cure a disease without side effects. Over time, it expanded to describe any seemingly simple, effective solution.

Example: They thought the new software would be a magic bullet for all their operational issues, but it didn't solve everything.

Make Someone's Blood Boil

Meaning: To make someone extremely angry or agitated.

Origin: In the past, scientists believed that blood boiled in the body when people were angry or excited. The term "the blood boils" has been used since the 1600s to mean "one gets angry," but the idiom "make someone's blood boil" didn't appear in print until 1848. Think of someone witnessing an act of injustice or experiencing a profound betrayal. Their anger might feel so intense, so consuming, that it feels as though their blood is literally boiling within them. This vivid imagery emphasizes the powerful and often overwhelming nature of extreme anger, highlighting the physical and emotional turmoil that can accompany such intense emotions.

Example: His rude comments made my blood boil, and I had to walk away to cool down.

Middle of the Road

Meaning: To adopt a position or attitude that avoids extremes, representing balance or moderation.

Origin: The phrase "middle of the road" originated in the United States in the 1890s. The earliest known use of the phrase was in 1891 in *Overland Monthly*. "Middle of the road" is used to describe something or someone that is ordinary, unexciting, or neither left-wing nor right-wing. For example, you might describe a policy as middle-of-the-road if it is not extreme or biased towards either the left or right. Whether it's political views, personal choices, or approaches to problem-solving, "middle-of-the-road" describes a balanced and moderate stance that seeks to avoid extremes and find common ground.

Example: Her political views are middle of the road, appealing to a wide range of people.

Monkey See, Monkey Do

Meaning: Imitating someone else's actions, often without understanding the reasoning behind them.

Origin: "Monkey See, Monkey Do" is a saying that originated in Jamaica in the early 18th century and popped up in American culture in the early 1920s. The saying refers to learning something by mimicry, without understanding why it works or being concerned about the consequences. "Monkey see, monkey do" highlights the powerful influence of observation and the tendency to learn through imitation, both in animals and in humans. Children, for example, often learn by observing and imitating the behavior of their parents, siblings, and peers. While imitation can be a valuable learning tool, the phrase also carries a subtle warning. It suggests that blindly following others without critical thinking can lead to undesirable consequences. It encourages us to observe, analyze, and learn from the actions of others, but also to think critically and make our own informed decisions.

Example: Little Timmy started using big words he didn't understand because he saw his older brother doing it—classic monkey see, monkey do behavior.

N

No Pain, No Gain

Meaning: Success requires hard work, effort, and sometimes suffering.

Origin: While the phrase "no pain, no gain" is commonly associated with Jane Fonda's 1980s aerobics videos, the concept itself is much older, with roots in the saying "there are no gains without pains" attributed to Benjamin Franklin. Essentially, significant achievement often requires hard work and discomfort to attain. This concept of "no pain, no gain" has extended beyond the realm of sports to encompass various aspects of life. It suggests that achieving any worthwhile goal, whether it's mastering a new skill, building a successful career, or overcoming personal challenges, often requires overcoming obstacles, enduring hardship, and pushing oneself beyond one's comfort zone. The phrase serves as a powerful motivator, encouraging us to persevere through challenges, to embrace discomfort, and to strive for excellence, knowing that true growth and achievement often come at a cost.

Example: You'll have to push through the tough workouts; remember, no pain, no gain!

No Time Like the Present

Meaning: There's no better time to do something than right now.

Origin: The saying "there's no time like the present" was first recorded in 1562. It's an idiom that means the best time to do something is right now. The saying is used to encourage someone to take action immediately instead of waiting. This proverb encourages us to embrace the present, to make the most of our opportunities, and to live life to the fullest. It's a reminder that procrastination can lead to missed opportunities and regrets, while taking action now can bring about positive change and fulfillment. The phrase "there's no time like the present" serves as a powerful motivator, urging us to seize the day, to pursue our goals, and to make the most of every moment.

Example: If you want to start that project, no time like the present—let's get started!

Not for All the Tea in China

Meaning: Not for anything in the world; something you wouldn't do, no matter the reward.

Origin: This idiom emphasizes the immense value of tea in 19th-century Europe, particularly in Britain. Tea from China was a highly prized commodity, considered a luxury item and a symbol of wealth and sophistication. The phrase "not for all the tea in China" suggests that something is so precious, so valuable, that it would not be exchanged for any amount of wealth or material possessions, not even for the vast quantities of tea that China could produce. The phrase "not for all the tea in China" has become a timeless idiom, a powerful way to express unwavering conviction and an absolute refusal to compromise on something that is deeply valued.

Example: I wouldn't go skydiving, not for all the tea in China!

Not My Cup of Tea

Meaning: Not something I enjoy or prefer; not to my liking.

Origin: This idiom has deep roots in British culture, where tea has long been a beloved and social beverage. Just as not everyone enjoys the same flavor of tea, the phrase "not my cup of tea" extends to describe any preference or taste that doesn't align with one's own. It's a polite and indirect way of expressing a dislike or disapproval for something. Whether it's a movie, a book, a hobby, or even another person, "not my cup of tea" allows one to express their disinterest without being overly critical or offensive. The phrase cleverly uses the familiar act of choosing and enjoying a beverage to express personal preference and disinclination, making it a concise and culturally relevant idiom.

Example: Opera isn't my cup of tea—I prefer rock music.

Not on My Watch

Meaning: Not while I'm in charge or responsible; something you won't allow to happen under your supervision.

Origin: This phrase originates from the military, specifically the concept of a "watch," which refers to a period of duty where a soldier or sailor is responsible for guarding a particular area or performing specific tasks. Imagine a sentry on guard duty, sworn to protect the fort from attack. Their primary responsibility is to ensure that no harm comes to the fort "on their watch." This sense of responsibility and vigilance is the very essence of the phrase. Today, "not on my watch" is used to express a strong determination to prevent something undesirable from happening. It can be used in various contexts, from a parent vowing to protect their children from harm to a leader vowing to prevent injustice within their community. The phrase emphasizes the importance of taking responsibility, of actively working to prevent negative outcomes, and of ensuring that things run smoothly while one is in charge.

Example: "If any of you are thinking of slacking off, not on my watch!"

Not the Sharpest Pencil in the Box

Meaning: Not very intelligent or quick-witted.

Origin: This idiom draws a humorous comparison between a person's intellect and the sharpness of a pencil. Just as a dull pencil struggles to write clearly and effectively, a person who is "not the sharpest pencil in the box" lacks mental acuity, quick wit, or intellectual sharpness. The image of a dull, blunt pencil, struggling to leave a mark, perfectly captures the feeling of someone who is not particularly intelligent or insightful. The phrase is often used in a lighthearted and humorous way, acknowledging someone's limitations in a gentle and good-natured manner. It's a reminder that intelligence comes in many forms, and that everyone has their own unique strengths and weaknesses.

Example: "He's not the sharpest pencil in the box, but he's got a good heart."

Not the Sharpest Tool in the Shed

Meaning: Not very intelligent or bright.

Origin: This idiom draws a humorous comparison between a person's intellect and the functionality of a tool. A shed typically contains a variety of tools, from sharp and effective ones like hammers and saws, to less useful or even broken ones. The phrase "not the sharpest tool in the shed" playfully suggests that someone is not the most intelligent or insightful individual, much like a dull tool is not the most effective for its intended purpose. It's important to note that this idiom is often used in a lighthearted and good-natured way, rather than as a serious insult. It's a gentle way to describe someone who may not be the most intellectually gifted, while acknowledging that everyone has their own unique strengths and weaknesses.

Example: "I wouldn't ask him for advice on that project—he's not the sharpest tool in the shed."

Not to Mince One's Words

Meaning: To speak directly and without hesitation, often in a blunt or honest manner.

Origin: This idiom evokes the image of finely chopping or "mincing" something, reducing it to small, less impactful pieces. Just as mincing meat changes its texture and diminishes its impact, "mincing words" implies softening or watering down one's message, making it less forceful or direct. "Not to mince one's words" suggests a direct and forthright style of communication, where one expresses their thoughts and opinions honestly and without reservation. It implies a willingness to speak one's mind, even if it means being blunt or potentially offending someone. This direct style of communication can be both refreshing and challenging. It allows for honest and open dialogue, but it also requires careful consideration and a willingness to accept the potential consequences of one's words.

Example: "When it comes to his opinion, he doesn't mince his words—he says exactly what's on his mind."

O

Off the Beaten Track

Meaning: Something unusual, not conventional, or away from the usual path.

Origin: This phrase originates from the concept of well-worn paths, the routes frequently traveled by people and animals. These "beaten tracks" represent the familiar, the conventional, and the well-traveled. "Off the beaten track" implies venturing away from these familiar paths, exploring the unknown, and seeking out something unique and unconventional. Whether it's a remote destination, an unusual hobby, or an unconventional approach to a problem, the phrase "off the beaten track" suggests a willingness to explore the unknown, to embrace the unique, and to seek out experiences that are less common and more authentic. This idiom encourages us to step outside our comfort zones, to embrace the unfamiliar, and to discover the hidden gems that lie beyond the well-trodden paths.

Example: We decided to take a trip off the beaten track and explore some remote villages.

Off the Record

Meaning: Information that is not meant to be made public or officially recorded.

Origin: The phrase "off the record" originated in the 1930s and was used to describe when someone did not want to be quoted by journalists. It may have come from the idea of removing irrelevant information from court records. The phrase is used to describe something that is said in confidence and is not intended to be published or officially noted. The concept of "off the record" has expanded beyond journalism to encompass any situation where information is shared confidentially, with the understanding that it will not be repeated or publicly disclosed. The phrase emphasizes the importance of trust and confidentiality in communication. It recognizes the value of private conversations and the need to respect the wishes of those who share information on a confidential basis.

Example: The CEO shared some confidential details with me, but it was all off the record.

Old Enough to Know Better

Meaning: Someone who should act more responsibly due to their age or experience.

Origin: This phrase implies that someone has reached an age or stage in life where they should possess a greater degree of wisdom, judgment, and self-control. It suggests that their actions or behavior are inappropriate for their age and experience, that they should know better than to engage in such behavior. For example, an adult throwing a temper tantrum might be told they are "old enough to know better." This phrase is often used to express disappointment or disapproval, implying that someone's actions are childish, irresponsible, or inconsistent with their age and level of maturity.

Example: You're old enough to know better than to leave your homework until the last minute!

Old Flame

Meaning: A former romantic partner or love interest.

Origin: The earliest known use of the idiom "old flame" to refer to a past romantic relationship was in the mid-1600s. The first recorded instance was in 1651, in the writing of Thomas Stanley, a poet and classical scholar. No individual is credited with the phrase's origin. It implies a past romantic connection that, though over, still holds a certain significance and may even evoke nostalgic feelings. The phrase "old flame" is often used to describe a former lover or romantic interest who may still hold a special place in one's heart, even if the relationship itself has long since ended.

Example: She bumped into her old flame at the reunion, and it brought back a lot of memories.

Old School/Skool

Meaning: Traditional, classic, or out-of-date methods, ideas, or styles.

Origin: The term "old school" originated in the mid-1700s and is a compound of the words "old" and "school." The earliest known use of the term was in 1749 in a translation by writer Tobias Smollett. "Old school" is a slang term that refers to something from an earlier era that is held in high regard or respect. It can be used as a noun or an adjective. For example, you might hear someone describe a classic rock band as "old school," a particularly rigorous teacher as "old school," or a vintage car as "old school." The phrase "old school" often carries a subtle sense of respect for tradition and a nostalgic appreciation for the past. It can also be used playfully to describe someone who is a bit set in their ways or prefers traditional methods.

Example: He's very old school when it comes to teaching; he prefers chalkboards over digital tools.

On Cloud Nine

Meaning: Feeling extremely happy or elated.

Origin: While there are a few theories about its origin, the most widely accepted one connects it to the *International Cloud Atlas*, published in 1896. This atlas classified clouds into ten different types, with cumulonimbus clouds, the highest and most dramatic type, often listed as number nine. These towering, fluffy clouds, reaching incredible heights, evoke a sense of awe and wonder. The image of floating on such a magnificent cloud, high above the world, perfectly symbolizes a state of pure bliss and contentment. Therefore, "on cloud nine" came to represent a feeling of overwhelming happiness, a state of euphoria where one feels light, carefree, and completely content. This association of the highest and most impressive cloud type with ultimate happiness has made "on cloud nine" a beloved idiom, used to describe feelings of intense joy and exhilaration.

Example: After hearing the news of her promotion, she was on cloud nine all day.

On Hand

Meaning: Available or present for a particular purpose or event.

Origin: The phrase "on hand" comes from the Middle English words *onhande* and *onhende*, which come from the Old English word *onhende*. *Onhende* means "on hand, demanding attention." The phrase is related to the Icelandic word *áhendur*, which means "within reach." "On hand" is an idiom that means something or someone is close by and can be used or is ready to help if needed. The phrase "on hand" emphasizes the importance of preparedness and the convenience of having necessary resources readily available when needed.

Example: The technician will be on hand to assist with the setup during the event.

On Pins and Needles

Meaning: Feeling nervous or anxious, often in anticipation of something.

Origin: This idiom originates from the uncomfortable sensation you experience when sitting on pins and needles. The sharp points of the pins create a tingling, uncomfortable feeling, making it difficult to relax and focus. This physical sensation of discomfort perfectly mirrors the emotional state of anxiety and nervousness. When someone is "on pins and needles," they are experiencing a heightened state of arousal, often due to anticipation, apprehension, or excitement. They may be waiting for important news, anticipating a challenging event, or simply feeling nervous in a social situation. Regardless of the specific cause, the phrase "on pins and needles" vividly captures the feeling of anxious anticipation and the discomfort that accompanies it.

Example: She was on pins and needles waiting for the results of her job interview.

On the Right Track

Meaning: Making progress in the right direction or doing something correctly.

Origin: This phrase likely comes from the literal idea of traveling along a railroad track. Just as a train traveling on the correct track is moving towards its intended destination, so too is someone "on the right track" making progress towards their goals. This vivid image of staying on course, of moving in the right direction, perfectly captures the essence of the idiom. It suggests that someone is making positive progress, that their efforts are leading them towards their desired outcome. It implies that someone is using the correct methods or strategies to achieve their goals. The phrase offers encouragement and reassurance, suggesting that someone is on the right path and that continued effort will likely lead to success. The phrase "on the right track" is a powerful motivator, offering encouragement and reassurance that one is moving in the right direction, even if the journey may still be long.

Example: Keep up the good work, you're on the right track to meeting your goals.

On the Same Wavelength

Meaning: Understanding or thinking in the same way as someone else.

Origin: Just as radio waves must be tuned to the same frequency to receive the same signal, two people "on the same wavelength" are able to understand and connect with each other effortlessly. They easily grasp each other's thoughts, feelings, and intentions. Communication flows smoothly, with minimal need for explanation or clarification. There's a sense of harmony and connection, a feeling of being in sync with the other person. For example, two close friends might be "on the same wavelength," finishing each other's sentences or anticipating each other's needs. The phrase emphasizes the importance of shared understanding and mutual respect in any successful relationship, whether it's a personal, professional, or creative partnership.

Example: We were on the same wavelength during the meeting and came up with great ideas.

On Thin Ice

Meaning: In a risky or precarious situation, where things could go wrong at any moment.

Origin: This idiom originated from the danger of breaking through thin ice and falling into water. American poet and essayist Ralph Waldo Emerson first used the phrase figuratively in his 1841 essay, *Prudence*: "In skating over thin ice our safety is in our speed." The phrase "on thin ice" serves as a powerful reminder of the importance of caution and careful consideration when navigating uncertain or risky situations.

Example: You'll be on thin ice if you keep ignoring the company rules.

One for the Road

Meaning: A final drink or indulgence before leaving or ending an event.

Origin: The phrase refers to a final drink before leaving a place, and it originated from a practice in the Middle Ages.

Example: Let's have one for the road before we call it a night.

Out in the Open

Meaning: Something that is revealed, public, or no longer hidden.

Origin: This phrase dates back to the early 19th century and draws its origin from the concept of secrecy versus disclosure. It perfectly captures the idea of something that is no longer hidden or concealed. It evokes the image of something that was previously kept secret or hidden from view, now brought into the light of day. Just as something brought out into the open air is exposed to the elements and visible to all, a secret that is "out in the open" is now public knowledge, exposed to scrutiny. This shift from secrecy to openness can have a variety of implications. It can bring about a sense of relief, as the burden of keeping a secret is lifted. However, it can also lead to embarrassment, shame, or even legal consequences. The phrase "out in the open" emphasizes the importance of transparency and honesty. While keeping secrets can sometimes be necessary, there are times when bringing things "out in the open" can lead to greater clarity, understanding, and ultimately, resolution.

Example: The secret is out in the open now that the announcement has been made.

Out of Line

Meaning: Acting inappropriately or outside the accepted norms.

Origin: This idiom originates from the concept of staying within a designated line, whether it's a physical line in a formation or a figurative line of acceptable behavior. Stepping "out of line" implies a transgression, a violation of established rules or expectations. Imagine soldiers marching in formation. Any deviation from the straight line, any individual stepping out of place, disrupts the order and unity of the group. This image of disrupting order and transgressing boundaries perfectly mirrors the metaphorical meaning of the phrase. "Out of line" describes behavior that is considered inappropriate, disrespectful, or unacceptable within a particular context. It can refer to anything from making rude comments to breaking the rules, from violating social norms to exceeding one's authority. The phrase emphasizes the importance of adhering to established rules and expectations, respecting boundaries, and behaving in a manner that is considerate of others.

Example: His behavior during the meeting was completely out of line, and it upset everyone.

Out of the Gate

Meaning: Starting something quickly or with great energy from the beginning.

Origin: The idiom "out of the gate" originated from horse racing, where starting gates are used to contain horses before a race. When the gates open, the horses burst out, starting the race. This image of a powerful and rapid start perfectly mirrors the metaphorical meaning of the phrase. "Out of the gate" describes any situation where someone or something begins with great energy, enthusiasm, and a strong initial momentum. The phrase "out of the gate" emphasizes the importance of a strong and decisive beginning. It suggests that a successful outcome is often determined by the initial burst of energy, the momentum generated at the very start.

Example: She came out of the gate with a bold new idea that impressed everyone in the room.

Over the Moon

Meaning: Extremely happy or delighted.

Origin: This evocative idiom likely originates from the nursery rhyme "Hey Diddle Diddle," which famously includes the line "The cow jumped over the moon." This whimsical image of a cow performing an extraordinary feat, soaring above the moon, has come to symbolize a state of pure joy and exhilaration. Just as the cow in the nursery rhyme defies gravity and reaches unimaginable heights, someone who is "over the moon" is experiencing a level of happiness that surpasses ordinary human emotions. They are filled with joy, excitement, and a sense of wonder, their spirits soaring to new heights. The phrase "over the moon" is a vivid and universally understood expression that perfectly encapsulates the feeling of overwhelming happiness and contentment.

Example: When he found out he had been accepted into his dream school, he was over the moon.

P

Paint the Town Red

Meaning: To go out and celebrate in a lively, extravagant way.

Origin: The origin of this phrase is often attributed to the notorious exploits of the Third Marquess of Waterford and his companions in the 19th century. Legend has it that this boisterous group, after a night of heavy drinking, embarked on a spree of mischief, painting various landmarks and buildings in the town of Melton Mowbray, England, a vibrant shade of red. This legendary night of revelry, marked by boisterous behavior and a disregard for convention, has become synonymous with a night of wild partying and exuberant celebration. Today, "painting the town red" evokes images of a lively night out, filled with laughter, music, and perhaps a few drinks. It suggests a night of unrestrained enjoyment, where social inhibitions are shed and a sense of carefree abandon takes over. The phrase has become a beloved idiom, capturing the essence of a truly memorable night out, a night where memories are made and the town, if only for a brief moment, is transformed by the vibrant energy of celebration.

Example: After completing the project, they decided to paint the town red and celebrate their success.

Paper Tiger

Meaning: A person or thing that appears threatening but is actually weak or harmless.

Origin: The phrase originated in China and was popularized by Chairman Mao Zedong in the mid-20th century. It refers to something or someone that appears to be powerful or threatening but is actually weak and ineffectual. The image of a paper tiger is quite telling – a tiger, a powerful and fearsome predator, is reduced to a mere imitation, a harmless object made of paper. This stark contrast perfectly captures the essence of the phrase. A paper tiger might seem intimidating at first glance, perhaps through bluster, threats, or a display of outward strength. However, upon closer examination, their true nature is revealed: weakness, ineffectiveness, and an inability to back up their threats with real power. The phrase "paper tiger" is often used to describe individuals, organizations, or even political entities that project an image of strength and power but ultimately lack the substance to back it up.

Example: Don't worry about his threats—he's just a paper tiger, all bark and no bite.

Pass with Flying Colors

Meaning: To succeed or complete something with great success, often with distinction.

Origin: The idiom "pass with flying colors" originated during the Age of Exploration, when ships would return to port with their flags raised or lowered to indicate success or defeat. This image of a ship returning home with its flags flying high, a testament to its success, perfectly captures the essence of the phrase. "Passing with flying colors" implies not just mere success, but a resounding triumph, a performance that surpasses expectations. Today, the phrase is used to describe any achievement that is accomplished with exceptional ease or brilliance. Whether it's passing an exam with a perfect score, delivering a captivating presentation, or achieving a personal goal with remarkable speed and efficiency, "passing with flying colors" signifies a resounding success, a victory that is celebrated with pride and admiration.

Example: She passed the exam with flying colors, earning top marks in every subject.

Pay Lip Service

Meaning: To express support or agreement verbally, without taking any real action.

Origin: The expression "pay lip service" originated in religious contexts, where it was used to describe prayers said out loud but not felt in the heart. The phrase began to be used in the 17th century and has since evolved to describe insincere support or hollow promises in various situations. Imagine someone expressing strong support for a cause but never actually volunteering their time or donating any money. This is a classic example of "paying lip service" – offering verbal support while remaining completely detached from any meaningful action. This phrase highlights the difference between genuine support and superficial approval. It serves as a reminder that true support requires more than just words; it requires action, commitment, and a willingness to contribute meaningfully to the cause. "Paying lip service" can be seen in various contexts, from political rhetoric to social interactions. It's a subtle criticism of those who offer empty promises and superficial support without any genuine intention to act.

Example: The company paid lip service to sustainability but didn't actually implement any green practices.

Pecking Order

Meaning: A hierarchy or ranking system, often based on power or status.

Origin: The phrase captures the concept of a hierarchical social structure. It originates from the observation of social behavior within flocks of chickens. Chickens, like many social animals, establish a clear dominance hierarchy. Higher-ranking chickens assert their dominance by pecking at lower-ranking chickens. This pecking order determines access to food, mates, and other resources. This observation of chicken behavior has been used to describe social hierarchies in humans. Just as there is a pecking order among chickens, there are often hierarchies within human groups, whether it's in a workplace, a social group, or even within a family. These hierarchies can be based on factors such as power, status, seniority, or social influence. The phrase "pecking order" effectively conveys the idea of a social hierarchy where individuals or groups compete for dominance and where there is a clear ranking system based on power and status.

Example: In the office, there's a clear pecking order, with the CEO at the top.

Phone Ringing Off the Hook

Meaning: Receiving a very high volume of phone calls, usually indicating high demand or popularity.

Origin: This vivid idiom originates from the days of landline telephones, where the receiver hung on a hook when not in use. When a call came in, the ringing would cause the receiver to swing wildly back and forth, sometimes even falling off the hook altogether. This image of a constantly ringing phone, with the receiver swinging wildly, perfectly captures the essence of the phrase. It evokes a sense of overwhelming demand, of being inundated with calls, and of struggling to keep up with the sheer volume of incoming communication. Today, while the technology has evolved, the meaning of the phrase remains the same. "Phone ringing off the hook" is used to describe any situation where there is an overwhelming demand for something, whether it's a popular product, a sought-after service, or even a celebrity attracting a large crowd of fans.

Example: Since the product launch, our phone has been ringing off the hook with inquiries.

Pie in the Sky

Meaning: A hopeful or unrealistic expectation that is unlikely to happen.

Origin: This idiom has a fascinating origin, stemming from the labor movement in the early 20th century. The phrase was popularized by the song "The Preacher and the Slave," written by the labor activist Joe Hill. In this song, Hill satirized the idea of religious promises of heavenly rewards in the afterlife, comparing them to an elusive "pie in the sky." This metaphorical use of "pie in the sky" effectively conveyed the idea of a distant and unattainable reward, something that is promised but never truly delivered. Today, "pie in the sky" is used to describe any unrealistic or overly optimistic expectation. It can refer to unrealistic promises, unattainable goals, or any idea that seems more like a fantasy than a realistic possibility. The phrase serves as a caution against unrealistic expectations and encourages us to focus on achievable goals and tangible rewards.

Example: His dream of becoming a millionaire overnight is just pie in the sky.

Pipe Down

Meaning: To be quiet or stop talking.

Origin: The expression "pipe down" originated in the nautical world as a signal from a boatswain's pipe to instruct the crew to be quiet or go below decks. It's a direct and often informal way of telling someone to be quiet, whether it's during a conversation, in a public space, or in any situation where excessive noise is disruptive. The phrase "pipe down" is a concise and effective way to request silence, a reminder to be mindful of others and to avoid unnecessary noise.

Example: The teacher told the students to pipe down so they could start the lesson.

Play Hard to Get

Meaning: To act as though you're not interested in someone, often in a romantic context, to make them more eager.

Origin: This intriguing phrase originates from the realm of courtship and romantic relationships. It describes a strategy where someone deliberately acts less interested or enthusiastic than they truly are in order to pique the other person's interest. The idea is that by appearing less available or less eager, one can make themselves seem more desirable. This can create a sense of challenge and intrigue, making the other person work harder to gain their attention and affection. While the effectiveness of this strategy is debatable, "playing hard to get" remains a common social phenomenon, reflecting the complexities of human interaction and the often-subtle dynamics of attraction. It's important to note that this strategy can sometimes backfire, leading to confusion, frustration, or even a loss of interest.

Example: She's playing hard to get, but I'm sure she likes him.

Play to the Gallery

Meaning: To act in a way that is intended to get approval or applause from an audience, often without regard for substance.

Origin: The phrase originates from theater, specifically referring to the cheapest seats in the theater, often located in the upper balconies. These seats were typically occupied by a less discerning audience, more interested in spectacle and sensationalism than in nuanced or sophisticated performances. Actors who "played to the gallery" would often exaggerate their emotions, engage in overly dramatic gestures, and prioritize crowd-pleasing antics over genuine artistic expression. This focus on immediate approval and audience gratification, rather than on artistic integrity, perfectly captures the essence of the phrase. Today, "playing to the gallery" is used to describe any situation where someone prioritizes applause, popularity, or public approval over substance or genuine merit. It can refer to politicians making empty promises, artists compromising their artistic vision for commercial success, or anyone who prioritizes external validation over personal integrity.

Example: His speech was just playing to the gallery, saying whatever would get the loudest applause.

Pot Calling the Kettle Black

Meaning: Accusing someone of something you are guilty of yourself.

Origin: This phrase dates back to the 1600s and refers to the blackened appearance of old cooking pots and kettles, which would become blackened from soot over time. If one pot were to criticize another for being "black," the accusation would be quite ironic, as both are equally stained by the cooking process. This simple observation of everyday life has become a powerful metaphor for hypocrisy. When someone criticizes another for a fault that they themselves possess, they are essentially "the pot calling the kettle black." The phrase highlights the importance of self-awareness and the irony of criticizing others for flaws that we may possess ourselves. It serves as a reminder to be mindful of our own shortcomings before pointing fingers at others.

Example: He criticized her for being late again, but that's the pot calling the kettle black!

Prick Up One's Ears

Meaning: To listen attentively or become alert, usually to something of interest.

Origin: This idiom comes from the way animals, particularly dogs or cats, raise their ears when they hear something interesting or out of the ordinary. This physical action, of raising the ears to improve hearing, is the very essence of the idiom. This image of heightened awareness, of focusing one's attention on a particular sound or stimulus, perfectly mirrors the metaphorical meaning of the phrase. When someone "pricks up their ears," they become suddenly alert and attentive. They may be listening intently to a conversation, trying to overhear a piece of gossip, or simply responding to an unexpected sound. The phrase emphasizes the importance of active listening and the ability to quickly shift one's focus to something of interest.

Example: When he mentioned the new job opening, I pricked up my ears immediately.

Pros and Cons

Meaning: The positive and negative aspects of something.

Origin: "Pros" is from the Latin word *pro*, meaning "for," and "cons" comes from *contra*, meaning "against." The phrase was created to help weigh the benefits and drawbacks of a situation or decision. By carefully looking at both the "pros" and "cons" of a particular action, we can make better and more thoughtful decisions. This method helps us see the good and bad sides, so we can choose the best option for our needs and priorities.

The phrase "pros and cons" is now a common part of our everyday language. It's used in many situations, from personal decisions (like choosing a job or buying a house) to more complex topics like policy decisions and political debates.

Example: Before making the decision, let's list the pros and cons of moving to a new office building.

Pull One out of the Hat

Meaning: To do something surprising or unexpected, usually to resolve a problem.

Origin: This phrase comes from the classic magic trick of pulling a rabbit or other unexpected object out of a hat. This act of seemingly creating something from thin air creates a sense of wonder and surprise. Just as a magician amazes the audience with an impossible feat, "pulling something out of the hat" refers to any situation where someone unexpectedly finds a solution, comes up with a creative idea, or overcomes a challenge in a surprising way. It suggests creativity, resourcefulness, and sometimes even a bit of luck, as if the solution appeared magically. For example, a team facing a tight deadline might "pull a rabbit out of the hat" by finding a creative solution to meet their deadline.

Example: He managed to pull one out of the hat by presenting a brilliant solution to the crisis.

Pull the Plug

Meaning: To stop or end something, especially a project, plan, or system.

Origin: This phrase comes from the act of pulling the plug on a machine, especially life-support systems in hospitals, to stop them from working. In this critical situation, "pulling the plug" means the difficult decision to end life-sustaining treatment, effectively ending the patient's life. This strong image of ending something suddenly has extended beyond the medical context. Today, "pull the plug" is used to describe ending or stopping anything, from a failed project to a disappointing relationship.

Example: After months of poor sales, the company decided to pull the plug on the new product line.

Pushing up Daisies

Meaning: A euphemism for being dead and buried.

Origin: This phrase comes from the idea that when someone is buried, flowers like daisies grow above their grave. It creates a gentle and somewhat whimsical image of death, connecting it to the natural cycle of life where the deceased returns to the earth and becomes part of the natural world. The image of daisies growing over a grave, symbolizing rebirth and renewal, softens the harsh reality of death, creating a more gentle and accepting perspective. "Pushing up daisies" is a euphemism that allows us to talk about death in a less morbid and more accepting way. It acknowledges the inevitability of death while also emphasizing the cycle of life and nature's ongoing renewal.

Example: One day we'll all be pushing up daisies, so we should live life to the fullest.

Put a Spoke in Someone's Wheel

Meaning: To disrupt or hinder someone's plans or progress.

Origin: This idiom comes from the concept of a wagon wheel. Spokes are important parts of a wheel, allowing it to turn smoothly. However, if a spoke is put into the wheel, it can stop it from turning, causing it to slow down or even stop completely. "Putting a spoke in someone's wheel" describes any action that intentionally stops or slows someone's progress. This could mean spreading rumors, sabotaging their efforts, or creating obstacles that make it hard for them to succeed. The phrase highlights the deliberate effort to stop someone's plans and prevent them from achieving their goals.

Example: His suggestion really put a spoke in our wheel, delaying the project by weeks.

Put One's Thinking Cap on

Meaning: To start thinking seriously or to concentrate on a problem.

Origin: The idiom "put on one's thinking cap" originated in the late 1800s and means to think or reflect seriously about something. This imaginary headgear symbolizes the act of shifting into a more focused and analytical mindset. "Putting on your thinking cap" implies a conscious effort to engage in deep thought, to approach a problem with seriousness and attention. It suggests a shift from casual thinking to a more deliberate and analytical mode of thought. This metaphorical "thinking cap" encourages us to approach challenges with greater focus, to think critically, and to utilize our cognitive abilities to their fullest extent.

Example: We need to put our thinking caps on to come up with a solution to this issue.

R

Rain on Someone's Parade

Meaning: To spoil someone's enjoyment or plans.

Origin: The phrase likely evokes the image of a joyous parade suddenly interrupted by a downpour of rain. The lively music and vibrant colors are muted, the celebratory spirit dampened, and the parade itself may even be forced to come to a halt. This image of a sudden and unwelcome disruption perfectly mirrors the metaphorical meaning of the phrase. "Raining on someone's parade" describes any action or statement that spoils someone's happiness or enthusiasm. The phrase "rain on someone's parade" highlights the importance of considering the impact of our words and actions on others, especially when they are experiencing joy and excitement.

Example: I didn't want to rain on his parade, but I had to tell him the news.

Raise the Bar

Meaning: To set a higher standard or expectation.

Origin: This idiom comes from competitive sports, specifically high jump and pole vault competitions. In these events, the bar is gradually raised higher and higher, challenging the athletes to jump further and achieve greater heights. This image of progressively increasing the level of difficulty perfectly mirrors the metaphorical meaning of the phrase. "Raising the bar" implies setting higher standards, pushing boundaries, and striving for greater achievement. The phrase "raise the bar" encourages us to strive for excellence, to push our limits, and to continually seek ways to improve and achieve greater heights.

Example: The company raised the bar for customer service with its new training program.

Raring to Go

Meaning: Eager and excited to begin something.

Origin: The phrase captures the feeling of eagerness and excitement to begin something. It evokes the image of a horse rearing up on its hind legs, its muscles tense, and its energy palpable. This powerful display of energy and anticipation perfectly mirrors the feeling of being ready to embark on a new endeavor. "Raring to go" describes a state of high excitement and readiness. It suggests that someone is eager to begin, that they are brimming with enthusiasm and eager to put their plans into action. Whether it's an athlete preparing for a race, a student eager to start a new school year, or an entrepreneur launching a new business venture, "raring to go" captures the feeling of anticipation and the desire to get started. The phrase emphasizes the importance of enthusiasm and motivation in achieving success. It suggests that a strong start, fueled by excitement and determination, is often crucial for achieving one's goals.

Example: "After the long wait, I'm raring to go on this new project!"

Read the Riot Act

Meaning: To reprimand or warn someone sternly.

Origin: The phrase comes from the English Riot Act of 1714, which gave authorities the power to disperse unlawful assemblies. This act required a magistrate to read a proclamation aloud, warning the assembled crowd that their continued gathering was illegal and that they could face severe consequences if they did not disperse immediately. This historical context, where the reading of a specific act of Parliament served as a stern warning, is the foundation of the idiom. Today, "reading the riot act" is used to describe any situation where someone delivers a strong reprimand or warning. It implies a serious and forceful rebuke, often delivered in a stern and uncompromising tone. Whether it's a parent scolding a child, a boss reprimanding an employee, or a coach admonishing a team, "reading the riot act" signifies a serious rebuke and a clear expectation of improved behavior.

Example: The manager read the riot act to the team after the missed deadline.

Red Herring

Meaning: A misleading clue or distraction that misguides attention away from the real issue.

Origin: The term comes from the practice of fox hunting, where a smoked herring (which has a very strong and distinctive odor) was sometimes dragged across the trail to confuse and mislead the hounds. This practice, known as "trailing," was used to test the hounds' ability to follow the actual scent of the fox despite the distraction. This image of a misleading scent, deliberately used to divert attention from the true objective, perfectly mirrors the metaphorical meaning of the phrase. Today, "red herring" is used to describe any clue or piece of information that is intentionally or unintentionally misleading. The phrase "red herring" serves as a reminder of the importance of critical thinking and the need to carefully evaluate information to avoid being misled.

Example: The detective knew the broken window was a red herring, distracting them from the real culprit.

Rest Assured

Meaning: To be certain or confident that something will happen or is true.

Origin: The phrase has been used since the 1600s, with "assured" meaning "to make secure." When you tell someone to "rest assured," you are essentially saying that they should have no doubts or worries, that everything will be taken care of. The phrase implies a sense of security and confidence, as if you are providing a guarantee or a promise. It's often used to alleviate someone's anxiety or to provide comfort in a difficult situation. The phrase "rest assured" is a powerful way to offer comfort and support, to alleviate someone's worries, and to instill a sense of confidence and security.

Example: Rest assured, we will take care of everything for you.

Resting on One's Laurels

Meaning: To become complacent or inactive after achieving success.

Origin: In ancient Greece, victorious athletes and military leaders were crowned with laurel wreaths. Laurels are evergreen trees with fragrant leaves, and the wreath symbolized victory and honor. However, simply resting on one's laurels, basking in the glory of past achievements, can lead to stagnation and decline. This image of resting on past laurels, without striving for further accomplishments, perfectly mirrors the metaphorical meaning of the phrase. "Resting on one's laurels" describes the dangerous tendency to become complacent after achieving success. It warns against the dangers of complacency, emphasizing the importance of continuous effort, innovation, and the pursuit of new goals. The phrase serves as a reminder that past achievements, while valuable, should not be seen as an excuse to stop striving for improvement and to continue to push boundaries and seek new challenges.

Example: He's been resting on his laurels since his last promotion, but it's time for him to take on new challenges.

Ride Out the Storm

Meaning: To endure a difficult situation or time without giving up.

Origin: This idiom has its roots in the maritime world, where sailors would encounter storms at sea. To "ride out the storm" meant to weather the storm, to endure the strong winds and rough seas, and to ultimately survive the ordeal. This image of enduring a powerful and potentially destructive force, of weathering the storm and emerging safely on the other side, perfectly mirrors the metaphorical meaning of the phrase. Today, "ride out the storm" is used to describe the ability to endure any difficult situation, whether it's a personal crisis, a financial hardship, or a challenging period in one's life. It emphasizes the importance of resilience, perseverance, and the ability to withstand adversity. The phrase encourages us to remain strong and steadfast during challenging times, to weather the storm and emerge stronger on the other side.

Example: We'll need to ride out the storm of criticism and stay focused on our goal.

Right off the Bat

Meaning: Immediately or without delay.

Origin: This idiom comes from the sport of baseball, where a bat hits the ball right at the start of a game or play. This swift and immediate action is the core of the phrase. This image of immediate and decisive action perfectly mirrors the metaphorical meaning of the idiom. "Right off the bat" is used to describe anything that happens quickly, unexpectedly, or without any delay.

Example: She impressed us right off the bat with her innovative ideas.

Rip off the Band-Aid

Meaning: To do something difficult or painful quickly in order to get it over with.

Origin: The phrase refers to the experience of removing an adhesive bandage. Slowly peeling off a Band-Aid can cause a significant amount of pain and discomfort. However, ripping it off quickly, although initially painful, often minimizes the overall discomfort. This image of confronting a painful situation directly, rather than prolonging the inevitable, perfectly mirrors the metaphorical meaning of the phrase. The phrase "rip the Band-Aid off" encourages a decisive and direct approach to difficult situations, emphasizing the importance of facing challenges head-on rather than prolonging the inevitable.

Example: I didn't want to tell him, but I had to rip off the Band-Aid and break the news.

Rome Wasn't Built in a Day

Meaning: Important things take time and effort to achieve.

Origin: This is a timeless proverb that emphasizes the importance of patience and perseverance. The phrase highlights the fact that building a great city like Rome, with its magnificent architecture, intricate infrastructure, and rich history, was not accomplished overnight. It was the result of centuries of dedicated effort, countless contributions, and a gradual, continuous process of growth and development. This historical fact serves as a powerful metaphor for any significant undertaking. It reminds us that achieving great things often requires sustained effort, consistent dedication, and a long-term perspective. "Rome wasn't built in a day" encourages us to be patient and persistent in our pursuits, to embrace the journey, and to understand that significant accomplishments rarely happen overnight.

Example: Don't rush the project; remember, Rome wasn't built in a day!

Rough It

Meaning: To endure difficult or uncomfortable living conditions, often when camping or in basic environments.

Origin: The phrase likely originates from the experiences of early pioneers, explorers, and travelers who ventured into the wilderness.

These individuals often faced harsh conditions, lacking the comforts of modern civilization. They might have slept on the ground, cooked over an open fire, and endured inclement weather. This experience of living without modern conveniences, of enduring hardship and discomfort, is the essence of "roughing it."

Example: We had to rough it during our camping trip, with no electricity or running water.

Rub Elbows With

Meaning: To associate or interact with someone, often in a social or professional setting.

Origin: The phrase comes from the image of being in a crowded situation, where people are closely packed together and inevitably brushing shoulders or "rubbing elbows." This physical proximity symbolizes close interaction and social engagement. "Rubbing elbows" implies a degree of social interaction, a chance to meet and interact with people, often in a social or professional context. It suggests a situation where there is close contact and opportunities for networking and social engagement.

Example: At the gala, she had the chance to rub elbows with some of the city's most influential leaders.

Rubber Check

Meaning: A check that cannot be processed due to insufficient funds in the account.

Origin: The term cleverly uses the properties of rubber to illustrate its meaning. Rubber is known for its elasticity and flexibility, able to bend and bounce back to its original shape. Similarly, a "rubber check" is essentially worthless. It bounces back, just like a rubber ball, because there are insufficient funds in the account to cover the amount. The metaphor emphasizes the lack of substance and the illusory nature of the check. It's a clever way to describe a promise or guarantee that ultimately proves to be empty and worthless.

Example: I'm afraid the company gave us a rubber check, and we couldn't deposit it.

Rule the Roost

Meaning: To be the dominant or controlling person in a situation or group.

Origin: This idiom likely originates from the observation of social hierarchy within a flock of chickens. In a chicken coop, the rooster, or cockerel, is the dominant male. He establishes his authority through displays of aggression, protecting the hens and asserting his dominance over other roosters. This image of the rooster as the undisputed leader of the flock perfectly mirrors the metaphorical meaning of the phrase. "Rule the roost" describes someone who is in charge, who dominates a situation or group, and whose decisions are typically followed by others.

Example: In the office, she definitely rules the roost when it comes to decision-making.

Run Amuck

Meaning: To behave in a frenzied, chaotic, or uncontrolled manner.

Origin: The phrase originates from the Malay word "amok," which describes a dissociative state characterized by sudden and violent outbursts of aggression. In this state, individuals might run through a village or community, attacking people and objects indiscriminately. This image of frenzied and uncontrollable behavior, often involving violence and destruction, perfectly mirrors the metaphorical meaning of the phrase. Today, "run amuck" is used to describe any situation characterized by wild, uncontrolled, and often destructive behavior.

Example: The children were running amuck in the playground, shouting and playing wildly.

Run of the Mill

Meaning: Ordinary, average, or unremarkable.

Origin: The phrase originates from the world of manufacturing, specifically from the production lines of mills. In a mill, a "run" refers to a batch of goods produced in a single production cycle. The "run of the mill" products are the standard, average items produced during this process—nothing special, just the typical output. This image of mass-produced, ordinary goods perfectly mirrors the metaphorical meaning of the phrase. "Run of the mill" is used to describe anything that is commonplace, average, or unremarkable.

Example: The restaurant's menu was nice, but the food was just run of the mill—nothing special.

S

Save One's Bacon

Meaning: To rescue someone from a difficult or dangerous situation.

Origin: While the exact origin is debated, one popular theory suggests that "bacon" was once a slang term for one's body or life. In the 16th and 17th centuries, bacon was a valuable food source, representing sustenance and survival. Metaphorically, "saving someone's bacon" thus came to symbolize rescuing them from a perilous situation, much like saving a valuable commodity from destruction. Today, the phrase is used to describe any situation where someone is rescued from a difficult or dangerous situation.

Example: The quick-thinking firefighter saved my bacon when the building started to collapse.

Saving for a Rainy Day

Meaning: To put money aside for future difficulties or emergencies.

Origin: The idiom "save for a rainy day" can be traced back to the mid-1500s, originating from an Italian play called "La Spiritata" written by A. F. Grazzini. The play was later translated into English by John Lyly and renamed "The Bugbears," where the phrase appeared as, "Wold he haue me kepe nothing against a raynye day?" This practical necessity of preparing for times of hardship evolved into the metaphorical meaning of the phrase. "Saving for a rainy day" now refers to the wise practice of setting aside money, resources, or even time for unexpected events or challenging times.

Example: I've been saving for a rainy day in case I lose my job.

Scratch My Back and I'll Scratch Yours

Meaning: A mutual agreement where one person helps another with the expectation of receiving help in return.

Origin: The phrase originates from the simple act of scratching someone's back. It's a common gesture of goodwill, where one person performs a small favor for another with the expectation of receiving a similar favor in return. This simple act of reciprocal assistance perfectly mirrors the metaphorical meaning of the phrase. "Scratching someone's back" implies offering help or assistance with the understanding that they will reciprocate in kind.

In professional relationships, colleagues may help each other out with projects, expecting similar assistance in the future. In social interactions, friends may help each other with chores, run errands, or offer support during difficult times. In political alliances, political parties may form alliances, supporting each other's agendas in exchange for reciprocal support.

The phrase "scratch my back and I'll scratch yours" emphasizes the importance of reciprocity and mutual cooperation in human relationships. It acknowledges that helping others can be beneficial, as it often leads to reciprocal support and creates stronger, more mutually beneficial relationships.

Example: I helped him with his presentation, and now he's scratching my back by recommending me for the promotion.

Sea Change

Meaning: A profound or significant transformation.

Origin: The phrase "sea change" is derived from the imagery of a body undergoing a dramatic transformation through the forces of the sea, perfectly encapsulating the metaphorical meaning of "sea change." Today, "sea change" is used to describe any significant and transformative change, often one that affects society or culture as a whole. The phrase "sea change" emphasizes the profound and often unpredictable nature of significant transformations, highlighting their transformative power and their ability to reshape our understanding of the world.

Example: The new CEO brought a sea change to the company's culture.

See a Man About a Dog

Meaning: A vague or humorous way of saying you need to leave or do something without explaining exactly what it is.

Origin: The phrase "See a man about a dog" is a classic example of British understatement, a humorous and vague way of excusing oneself from a conversation or situation without providing any real explanation. While its exact origin remains uncertain, it likely emerged in the 19th century as a polite and somewhat mysterious way to excuse oneself from a social engagement. The phrase cleverly avoids providing any specific details, allowing the speaker to maintain their privacy while politely extricating themselves from the situation. The humorous ambiguity of the phrase adds to its charm. It leaves the listener wondering about the nature of the "man" and the "dog," sparking curiosity and perhaps even a touch of playful speculation.

Today, "See a man about a dog" remains a popular and often humorous way to excuse oneself from a conversation or situation without revealing one's true intentions. It's a classic example of British wit, allowing for a degree of privacy and a touch of playful mystery.

Example: I'll be right back, I need to see a man about a dog.

Sell Like Hotcakes

Meaning: To sell very quickly and in large quantities.

Origin: This idiom originates from the observation of how quickly hotcakes (or pancakes) were sold at fairs, carnivals, and other public events in the 1800s. These freshly cooked treats, often served hot and fragrant, were highly popular and would often sell out quickly, as fast as they could be made. This image of something being sold rapidly, as quickly as hotcakes can be cooked and served, perfectly mirrors the metaphorical meaning of the phrase. Today, "sell like hotcakes" is used to describe anything that is in high demand and sells very quickly.

Example: The new smartphone is selling like hotcakes—stores can barely keep it in stock!

Set off on the Right/Wrong Foot

Meaning: To begin a relationship or endeavor in a positive or negative way.

Origin: This idiom draws upon the ancient superstition that stepping off with the right foot first brings good luck, while stepping off with the left foot is considered unlucky.

Starting on the Right Foot: This implies a positive and auspicious beginning, characterized by good fortune and success. It suggests that the initial steps were taken with confidence, grace, and positive energy.

Starting on the Wrong Foot: This implies a poor or inauspicious beginning, characterized by difficulties, setbacks, or misunderstandings. It suggests that the initial steps were taken with hesitation, awkwardness, or even missteps.

The phrase "set off on the right/wrong foot" emphasizes the importance of first impressions and the impact of initial actions on the overall outcome of an endeavor, whether it's a new relationship, a new job, or any other significant undertaking.

Example: We set off on the wrong foot, but after a few meetings, things improved.

Settle Down

Meaning: To become calm, stable, and often start a family or establish a home.

Origin: The phrase evokes the image of a nomadic lifestyle coming to an end, of finding a permanent home and establishing roots in a particular place. Just as a traveler might settle down in a new town, finding a place to live and build a life, so too can individuals "settle down" in other aspects of their lives. "Settling down" suggests a period of transition and growth, culminating in a state of stability, contentment, and fulfillment. It emphasizes the importance of finding a sense of place and purpose, of establishing roots and building a fulfilling life.

Example: After years of traveling, he decided it was time to settle down and start a family.

Shipshape

Meaning: Neat, tidy, or in perfect condition.

Origin: Originating from nautical terminology, "shipshape" originally described a ship that was meticulously maintained and prepared for sea. Every inch of the vessel had to be in order, with all equipment properly stowed, the decks scrubbed clean, and the sails and rigging in perfect condition. A shipshape vessel was not only aesthetically pleasing but also safe and efficient, ready to face any challenges at sea. This image of a well-maintained and efficient ship perfectly mirrors the metaphorical meaning of the phrase. Today, "shipshape" is used to describe anything that is neat, tidy, and in good order. The phrase "shipshape" emphasizes the importance of order, efficiency, and attention to detail. It suggests a state of preparedness and a commitment to maintaining a high level of organization and cleanliness.

Example: After hours of cleaning, the house was shipshape and ready for the guests.

Short Shrift

Meaning: To give little attention or sympathy to someone or something.

Origin: The phrase has a fascinating origin rooted in religious practice. "Shrift" originally referred to the confession of sins to a priest. In medieval times, condemned prisoners were often given "short shrift" – a brief and hurried confession before their execution. This historical context, where limited time was given for confession before a severe consequence, perfectly mirrors the metaphorical meaning of the phrase. Today, "short shrift" is used to describe any situation where someone or something is given little attention, consideration, or respect.

Example: The manager gave my proposal short shrift, dismissing it without consideration.

Show Someone the Door

Meaning: To ask someone to leave, often in an abrupt or dismissive manner.

Origin: The phrase "show someone the door" was first recorded in 1778 and is an idiom that means to tell someone to leave or make it clear that you want them to leave. This direct and often abrupt action of escorting someone to the door perfectly mirrors the metaphorical meaning of the phrase. "Showing someone the door" implies a clear and decisive dismissal, often conveying a sense of disapproval or displeasure.

Examples:

1. Dismissing an unwanted guest: "When the guest became increasingly disruptive, the host had to show him the door."

2. Firing an employee: "After repeated warnings, the company finally showed him the door."

3. Ending a conversation abruptly: "She felt uncomfortable with the conversation and decided to show him the door."

Silver Bullet

Meaning: A simple and seemingly magical solution to a complex problem.

Origin: The phrase "silver bullet" captures the idea of a quick and effective remedy for a challenging issue. Historically, silver bullets were believed to have the power to kill mythical creatures like werewolves, making them a symbol of a perfect solution to a formidable problem. This evocative idiom originates from folklore and literature, where the silver bullet was depicted as a rare and powerful tool that could solve even the most difficult challenges with ease. The concept of a single, miraculous solution has since entered common parlance to describe any highly effective answer to a complex issue. The image of a silver bullet provides a powerful metaphor for finding a straightforward and efficient solution to a problem that seems insurmountable. It suggests a sense of hope and certainty that a perfect remedy exists, even in the face of significant challenges.

Example: The new software update proved to be the silver bullet we needed to resolve all our technical issues.

Silver Lining

Meaning: A hopeful or positive aspect in an otherwise negative situation.

Origin: The phrase captures the idea of finding hope or positivity in a difficult or challenging situation. This evocative idiom originates from the observation that even the darkest clouds often have a silver lining – a thin, bright edge illuminated by the sun. This seemingly insignificant detail, a sliver of light against a backdrop of darkness, offers a glimmer of hope and a reminder that even in the midst of adversity, there is always the possibility of something positive. This image of finding hope in unexpected places perfectly mirrors the metaphorical meaning of the phrase. "Silver lining" refers to any positive aspect or benefit that can be found in a difficult or challenging situation.

Example: Even though we lost the game, the silver lining was that we learned a lot about teamwork.

Sink One's Teeth into Something

Meaning: To become deeply involved or engaged in something, especially with enthusiasm.

Origin: The phrase "sink one's teeth into" is a metaphor that means to become fully engaged in something, or to do something with great enthusiasm. The phrase is thought to have originated in the early 1900s. It alludes to an animal biting into its prey. "Sinking one's teeth into something" implies a level of passion, dedication, and enthusiasm that goes beyond mere participation. It suggests a deep involvement, a willingness to fully immerse oneself in the task at hand, and a desire to explore its depths.

Example: She was eager to sink her teeth into the new project and get started right away.

Sitting Pretty

Meaning: To be in a comfortable, secure, or fortunate situation.

Origin: The phrase likely originates from the image of someone comfortably seated, relaxed, and secure, without any immediate worries or concerns. This relaxed and secure posture perfectly mirrors the metaphorical meaning of the phrase.

"Sitting pretty" suggests a state of comfort, security, and contentment, often accompanied by a sense of having achieved success and overcome challenges. It implies a position of privilege and advantage, where one can relax and enjoy the fruits of their labor without facing any immediate difficulties.

Examples:

Financial Security: "After winning the lottery, she was sitting pretty for the rest of her life."

Professional Success: "With a successful business and a loving family, he was sitting pretty."

Comfortable Circumstances: "Living in a beautiful home with no financial worries, they were sitting pretty."

Skeleton in the Closet

Meaning: A hidden secret, especially one that is embarrassing or shameful.

Origin: The phrase evokes the chilling image of a literal skeleton hidden away in a closet, a macabre secret concealed from the public eye. This image of something hidden and potentially disturbing perfectly mirrors the metaphorical meaning of the phrase. "Skeleton in the closet" refers to any secret that is kept hidden from public view, often due to embarrassment, shame, or the fear of negative consequences.

Example: He has a skeleton in the closet that he's been hiding for years.

Sleeping with the Enemy

Meaning: To cooperate or make an alliance with someone who is considered an opponent or rival.

Origin: The phrase originates from the concept of betrayal and treachery. In wartime, "sleeping with the enemy" would have been considered a grave betrayal, a violation of loyalty and a serious threat to one's own side. This image of betrayal and collaboration with the opposition perfectly mirrors the metaphorical meaning of the phrase. Today, "sleeping with the enemy" is used to describe any situation where someone cooperates or forms an alliance with someone who is considered an opponent or rival. The phrase "sleeping with the enemy" emphasizes the controversial and often morally ambiguous nature of such alliances, highlighting the potential risks and betrayals that can arise from cooperating with one's rivals.

Example: By working with the competitor, he felt like he was sleeping with the enemy.

Smell Something Fishy

Meaning: To sense that something is suspicious or not right.

Origin: The phrase originates from the distinctive odor of spoiled fish. When fish begins to decay, it emits a strong and unpleasant smell that immediately signals that something is wrong. This association between a bad smell and something being wrong or deceptive perfectly mirrors the metaphorical meaning of the phrase. "Smelling something fishy" implies an intuitive sense that something is not as it seems, a feeling that something is wrong or deceptive, even if there's no concrete evidence.

Example: When I heard about the sudden change in plans, I started to smell something fishy.

Snake in the Grass

Meaning: A hidden danger or deceitful person who poses as a friend.

Origin: The phrase "snake in the grass" is a metaphor for a treacherous person and originated from a line written by the Roman poet Virgil in 37 BCE. "Snake in the grass" is used to describe any hidden danger or deceitful person, someone who appears to be a friend but is actually an enemy. It serves as a warning against trusting blindly and emphasizes the importance of being wary of hidden dangers and potential betrayals.

Example: He seemed friendly at first, but I soon realized he was a snake in the grass.

Snowed Under

Meaning: To be overwhelmed with work or responsibilities.

Origin: The phrase originates from the image of being buried under a heavy snowfall. Imagine being caught in a blizzard, with the snow piling up around you, making it difficult to move or even see. This image of being overwhelmed and buried by a large amount of something perfectly mirrors the metaphorical meaning of the phrase. "Snowed under" describes a situation where someone is overwhelmed with work, responsibilities, or other demands.

Example: I've been snowed under with emails all day—I'll need a few hours to catch up.

Son of a Gun

Meaning: A playful or affectionate way of referring to someone, often used in a light-hearted or teasing manner.

Origin: The phrase "son of a gun" has an interesting history. It likely originated in the 17th century among sailors, where "gun" was often used to refer to a cannon. Children born at sea, often aboard a ship, were sometimes jokingly referred to as "sons of the gun," a playful and informal way to acknowledge their unique circumstances. Over time, the phrase evolved from its literal meaning to become a more general term of endearment or mild surprise. It's often used in a lighthearted and affectionate manner, without any negative connotations. For example, you might say "Well, son of a gun!" in a playful way to express surprise or admiration at someone's achievement. While it might seem somewhat unconventional, the phrase has become a part of everyday language, often used to express a range of emotions from mild surprise to playful affection.

Example: That son of a gun beat me to the finish line!

Spellbound

Meaning: To be completely captivated or fascinated by something.

Origin: The phrase comes from the idea of being completely captivated or mesmerized by something. It evokes the image of being under a magical spell, enchanted and hypnotized, unable to look away or break free from its influence. Just as a person under a spell is completely under the control of the caster, someone who is "spellbound" is completely captivated by something – a performance, a story, a piece of art, or even another person. Their attention is completely absorbed, their senses captivated, and their ability to think or act independently temporarily suspended.

Example: The audience was spellbound by the magician's performance.

Spit It Out

Meaning: To tell someone something you have been hesitating to say.

Origin: The phrase evokes the image of spitting something out of one's mouth forcefully and decisively. This physical action, of expelling something quickly and forcefully, perfectly mirrors the metaphorical meaning of the phrase. "Spitting it out" implies that someone is hesitating to speak, perhaps due to nervousness, fear, or reluctance. It urges them to overcome their hesitation and express themselves directly and without further delay.

Example: Come on, spit it out—what's bothering you?

Stand One's Ground

Meaning: To maintain one's position or opinion, even when challenged or pressured.

Origin: This idiom likely originates from a military context, where soldiers are encouraged to hold their positions and not retreat, even when faced with opposition. The phrase has been used since at least the 17th century and conveys a sense of determination and resilience. Over time, "standing one's ground" evolved to mean holding firm in any situation of opposition or conflict.

Example: Despite the pressure from her colleagues, she stood her ground and defended her ideas.

Start from Scratch

Meaning: To begin something anew from the very beginning, without using anything that was prepared earlier.

Origin: This idiom comes from the world of sports, particularly racing, where the "scratch line" was the starting line scratched into the ground. The first recorded use of the phrase in print was in a cricketing manual from 1833, but it was likely in use earlier. It implies beginning from a point of no advantage, with no prior preparation or assistance.

Example: After the project failed, they had to start from scratch and come up with a new plan.

Step Up to the Plate

Meaning: To take responsibility for something, especially in a time of challenge or difficulty.

Origin: This phrase originates from baseball, where a batter steps up to home plate to take their turn at bat. The phrase began to be used toward the end of the 19th century, with the first recorded example from a newspaper in 1874. It conveys a sense of readiness and willingness to take on a challenge.

Example: When the team leader resigned, she stepped up to the plate and took on the leadership role.

Stick One's Neck Out

Meaning: To take a risk by saying or doing something that might be criticized.

Origin: This idiom likely originates from the imagery of a turtle or an animal with a long neck, sticking its neck out of its shell or hiding place, making itself vulnerable. The phrase has been in use since at least the early 20th century. "Sticking one's neck out" implies taking a risk, often for the benefit of others, and being exposed to potential criticism or danger.

Example: He decided to stick his neck out and propose a bold new strategy for the project.

Stir the Hornet's Nest

Meaning: To provoke trouble or create a commotion.

Origin: This idiom comes from the literal action of disturbing a hornet's nest, which results in angry hornets swarming and attacking. The phrase has been used since at least the late 19th century. "Stirring the hornet's nest" implies causing a disturbance or provoking a strong and potentially hostile reaction.

Example: Her controversial comments stirred the hornet's nest and caused an uproar in the community.

Straight from the Horse's Mouth

Meaning: To get information directly from the original or most reliable source.

Origin: This idiom comes from horse racing, where tips about which horse is likely to win were considered most reliable when coming directly from the stable or those who were closest to the horse, such as trainers or jockeys. The phrase has been in use since at least the early 20th century. "Straight from the horse's mouth" implies receiving information from a trustworthy and direct source.

Example: I heard it straight from the horse's mouth that the company is planning to launch a new product next month.

Straight Shooter

Meaning: A person who is honest and direct in their dealings and communication.

Origin: This idiom originates from the Old West, where being a "straight shooter" referred to someone who could shoot a gun accurately and reliably. Over time, it evolved to describe someone who is honest, straightforward, and trustworthy. The phrase has been used since at least the early 20th century.

Example: Everyone trusts him because he's a straight shooter who always tells the truth.

Stubborn as a Mule

Meaning: Extremely stubborn and unwilling to change one's mind or behavior.

Origin: This idiom comes from the reputation of mules, which are known for their stubbornness and reluctance to follow directions. The phrase has been in use since at least the early 19th century. "Stubborn as a mule" implies someone who is very determined and difficult to persuade or change.

Example: He's as stubborn as a mule and refuses to admit he's wrong, even when faced with evidence.

Sunny Disposition

Meaning: A cheerful and optimistic attitude or temperament.

Origin: The phrase "sunny disposition" likely originates from the comparison of a cheerful, positive personality to the brightness and warmth of the sun. Just as the sun brings light and warmth to the world, a person with a sunny disposition brings happiness and positivity to those around them. The exact origin of the phrase is unclear, but it has been used in English literature and speech for several centuries.

Example: She always has a sunny disposition, which makes her a joy to be around.

Sweat Like a Pig

Meaning: To sweat profusely.

Origin: Interestingly, the phrase "sweat like a pig" is a bit of a misnomer since pigs do not actually sweat much. The term is believed to have originated from the process of pig iron production, where the iron cools and solidifies, resembling a pig's shape. When the iron cools, it forms droplets on the surface that look like sweat. This imagery has led to the phrase being used to describe someone sweating heavily.

Example: After running five miles in the summer heat, I was sweating like a pig.

T

Tail Between One's Legs

Meaning: To feel ashamed, embarrassed, or defeated.

Origin: This idiom likely originates from the behavior of dogs and other animals that tuck their tails between their legs when they feel scared, ashamed, or submissive. The imagery of an animal displaying submission or defeat perfectly mirrors the metaphorical meaning of the phrase, describing someone who feels embarrassed or defeated.

Example: After losing the argument, he walked away with his tail between his legs.

Take a Load Off

Meaning: To sit down and relax, especially after a period of exertion.

Origin: The phrase "take a load off" likely originates from the literal idea of setting down a heavy load or burden and taking a rest. It suggests taking a break to relieve physical or mental stress. The exact origin of the phrase is unclear, but it has been commonly used in casual speech for many years.

Example: Come on in and take a load off—you've had a long day.

Take Five

Meaning: To take a short break, typically five minutes.

Origin: The phrase "take five" likely originates from the world of music and theater, where performers are often given five-minute breaks during rehearsals or performances. The exact origin is unclear, but it has been used in English since at least the mid-20th century. "Take five" suggests taking a brief pause to rest or refresh oneself.

Example: Let's take five before we continue with the next part of the meeting.

Take Someone to the Cleaners

Meaning: To cheat or take a lot of money from someone.

Origin: The phrase "take someone to the cleaners" likely originates from the early 20th century, around the 1920s, in the United States. The term "cleaners" suggests a thorough cleaning out, often used in the context of gambling or business deals where one party takes everything from the other. It conveys a sense of financial loss and being left with nothing.

Example: After the divorce, he was taken to the cleaners and lost almost everything.

Take Something Out on Someone

Meaning: To unfairly blame or punish someone for one's own problems or frustrations.

Origin: This idiom has been used since the early 20th century. The idea is to metaphorically "take out" one's anger, frustration, or stress on another person, even though they are not the cause of the problem. It's about displacing negative emotions onto someone else.

Example: I know you're stressed, but don't take it out on me.

Take the Cake

Meaning: To be the most outstanding in some negative quality; to be the worst or most extreme example of something.

Origin: This phrase dates back to the 19th century and likely originates from the practice of awarding cakes as prizes in competitions. The phrase "take the cake" suggests that something is so remarkable (often in a negative way) that it wins the prize.

Example: Her behavior at the party really took the cake—I've never seen anything like it.

Taken Aback

Meaning: To be surprised or shocked.

Origin: The phrase "taken aback" comes from the nautical term used in the 17th century when a ship's sails were suddenly pushed back by the wind, causing the ship to stop or reverse direction. This unexpected change mirrors the metaphorical meaning of being surprised or shocked.

Example: I was taken aback by his sudden announcement.

Talk Someone into Something

Meaning: To persuade or convince someone to do something.

Origin: This idiom has been used since the early 20th century. The idea is to engage in conversation to persuade someone, using words and arguments to convince them to take a particular action.

Example: "She talked him into going to the concert, even though he initially didn't want to go."

Taste of One's Own Medicine

Meaning: To experience the same unpleasant treatment that one has given to others.

Origin: This phrase originates from Aesop's fable "The Cobbler Turned Doctor," where a cobbler pretends to be a doctor and sells fake medicine. When he gets sick, he is given his own "medicine" as a form of poetic justice. The phrase has been in use since the early 19th century.

Example: "He was always criticizing others, but when he received criticism himself, he got a taste of his own medicine."

Test the Waters

Meaning: To try something out or explore a situation before committing to it.

Origin: This idiom likely originates from the practice of testing the temperature of the water with one's foot before jumping in to see if it is comfortable. The phrase has been used since the early 20th century and conveys the idea of cautiously trying something new to assess the situation before making a full commitment.

Example: He decided to test the waters by attending a few classes before enrolling in the full course.

That's the Way the Ball Bounces

Meaning: That's just the way things happen, often implying acceptance of a situation that cannot be changed.

Origin: This idiom likely comes from the unpredictable nature of how a ball bounces. The phrase suggests that some things are beyond our control and we must accept them as they come. It has been used since at least the mid-20th century.

Example: We didn't win the contract, but that's the way the ball bounces.

The Apple Doesn't Fall Far from the Tree

Meaning: Children often resemble their parents in behavior, character, or appearance.

Origin: This idiom likely originates from the imagery of an apple falling from a tree and landing close to it. The phrase suggests that children inherit traits from their parents. It has been used in English since at least the 18th century.

Example: He's just as talented as his father. The apple doesn't fall far from the tree.

The Big Picture

Meaning: The overall perspective or broad view of a situation.

Origin: The phrase "the big picture" comes from the idea of looking at a large image or scene to understand the overall context, rather than focusing on the small details. It has been used since the mid-20th century to describe taking a holistic view of a situation.

Example: Before making a decision, we need to look at the big picture and consider all the factors involved.

The Chips Are Down

Meaning: A critical or difficult situation where the outcome is uncertain.

Origin: This idiom likely comes from gambling, particularly poker, where "the chips are down" refers to a situation where a player has placed their bets and the stakes are high. The phrase has been used since the early 20th century to describe any high-stakes situation.

Example: When the chips are down, you really see who your true friends are.

The Golden Age

Meaning: A period of great success, prosperity, or achievement in a particular field or area.

Origin: The phrase "golden age" originates from ancient Greek and Roman mythology, where it referred to a mythical age of peace, prosperity, and happiness. The term has been used since at least the early 17th century to describe any period of great success and flourishing in various contexts, such as arts, literature, or civilization.

Example: The 1920s are often considered the golden age of jazz music.

The Jig is Up

Meaning: The deception or scheme has been exposed; the game is over.

Origin: This idiom dates back to the 18th century and is derived from the use of the word "jig" to mean a trick or deceitful scheme. When the "jig is up," it means that the trick has been discovered and there is no longer any chance of success or escape.

Example: The police found the stolen goods, so the jig is up for the thieves.

The Lion's Share

Meaning: The largest or most significant portion of something.

Origin: This idiom originates from one of Aesop's fables, where a lion takes the largest share of the spoils of a hunt, leaving little or nothing for the other animals. The phrase has been used since the early 17th century to describe the largest or most significant portion of something.

Example: He took the lion's share of the profits from the business deal.

The Middle of Nowhere

Meaning: A remote or isolated place far from civilization.

Origin: The phrase "the middle of nowhere" evokes the image of being in a place that is distant from populated or developed areas. It has been used since at least the late 19th century to describe a location that feels isolated and far removed from any significant landmarks or amenities.

Example: "The cabin was located in the middle of nowhere, surrounded by miles of wilderness."

The Upper Crust

Meaning: The highest social class or elite group within a society.

Origin: The phrase "the upper crust" originally referred to the topmost layer of a loaf of bread, which was considered the best and most desirable part. Over time, the term came to be used metaphorically to describe the highest social class. It has been in use since at least the early 19th century.

Example: "They were part of the upper crust of society, attending exclusive parties and events."

The World is Your Oyster

Meaning: You have the ability and opportunity to achieve great things or explore the world.

Origin: This idiom originates from William Shakespeare's play "The Merry Wives of Windsor," written in 1602. The character Pistol says, "Why, then the world's mine oyster, Which I with sword will open." The phrase suggests that the world is full of opportunities, and one just needs to seize them, much like opening an oyster to find a valuable pearl.

Example: With your skills and determination, the world is your oyster.

There's the Rub

Meaning: That's the problem or difficulty.

Origin: This idiom comes from William Shakespeare's play "Hamlet," written around 1600. In Hamlet's famous soliloquy, he says, "To sleep: perchance to dream: ay, there's the rub." In this context, "rub" refers to an obstacle or difficulty. The phrase has since been used to point out the main problem or challenge in a situation.

Example: We want to expand the business, but funding is limited—there's the rub.

Thick as Thieves

Meaning: Very close friends who share secrets and trust each other completely.

Origin: This idiom dates back to the early 19th century and likely originates from the idea that thieves, who must trust each other to commit crimes, form very close bonds. The phrase implies a deep level of friendship and loyalty.

Example: They've been best friends since childhood, as thick as thieves.

Thinking Outside the Box

Meaning: To think creatively and innovatively, beyond conventional boundaries.

Origin: The phrase "thinking outside the box" likely originates from a puzzle called the "nine dots puzzle," which challenges individuals to connect nine dots with four straight lines without lifting the pen. Solving the puzzle requires drawing lines outside the perceived boundaries of the box formed by the dots. The phrase gained popularity in the 1970s and 1980s in business and management contexts, encouraging innovative thinking.

Example: The marketing team needs to think outside the box to come up with a unique campaign.

Through Thick and Thin

Meaning: To remain loyal and supportive through good times and bad.

Origin: This idiom has been used since at least the 13th century and likely originates from the idea of navigating through dense forests (thick) and open areas (thin). It suggests enduring all kinds of challenges and remaining steadfast. The phrase has evolved to mean unwavering loyalty and support, regardless of circumstances.

Example: They've been together through thick and thin, always supporting each other.

Throw Down the Gauntlet

Meaning: To issue a challenge or dare someone.

Origin: This idiom originates from the medieval practice of knights throwing down their gauntlets (armored gloves) as a way of challenging someone to a duel. The act of throwing down the gauntlet signaled a formal challenge that had to be accepted or declined. This practice dates back to at least the 14th century.

Example: The CEO threw down the gauntlet, challenging the team to double their sales by the end of the year.

Throw Someone to the Lions

Meaning: To put someone in a difficult or dangerous situation, often without support.

Origin: This idiom likely originates from the ancient Roman practice of throwing Christians to lions as a form of public execution and entertainment. It conveys the idea of exposing someone to danger or criticism without protection. The phrase has been used since at least the late 19th century.

Example: They threw him to the lions by making him present the unpopular proposal alone.

Throwing Shade

Meaning: To subtly or indirectly criticize or insult someone.

Origin: The phrase "throwing shade" originated in the LGBTQ+ ballroom culture of the 1980s. It was popularized by the documentary "Paris Is Burning" (1990) and later entered mainstream usage. "Throwing shade" implies delivering a sly or understated insult, often in a clever or witty manner.

Example: She was definitely throwing shade when she commented on his outdated fashion sense.

Tick Off

Meaning: To make someone angry or annoyed.

Origin: The idiom "tick off" likely originates from the early 20th century and is an informal way of saying to irritate or upset someone. The exact origin is unclear, but the phrase suggests making someone so irritated that they feel as if they are being marked off a list.

Example: His constant interruptions during the meeting really ticked me off.

Tight as a Tick

Meaning: Very tight or secure, often used to describe a close bond or a tight-fitting object.

Origin: This idiom originates from the behavior of ticks, which attach themselves tightly to their hosts to feed. The phrase has been used since at least the 19th century to describe something that is very tight or secure, similar to how tightly a tick attaches itself.

Example: The lid on the jar was tight as a tick, and I couldn't open it.

Till the Cows Come Home

Meaning: For a very long time; indefinitely.

Origin: This idiom likely originates from the farming practice where cows are let out to pasture and return home only after a long time. Cows are known to take their time grazing and meandering, so the phrase "till the cows come home" conveys the idea of a prolonged period. The phrase has been in use since at least the early 19th century.

Example: You can argue with him till the cows come home, but he won't change his mind.

To Bandy Something About

Meaning: To discuss or mention something in a casual or careless way.

Origin: The phrase "bandy about" comes from an old tennis-like game called "bandy," where players hit a ball back and forth. The term evolved to mean tossing ideas or words back and forth in conversation. It has been used in this context since at least the 16th century.

Example: They've been bandying about the idea of a company retreat, but nothing is decided yet.

To Be in Someone's Black Book

Meaning: To be in disfavor with someone; to be on someone's bad side.

Origin: The phrase originates from the practice of keeping a "black book" or a list of those who have committed offenses or are in disfavor. It dates back to at least the 17th century and implies being on a list of people who are not well-liked or trusted.

Example: Ever since the argument, I've been in his black book.

To Be Left High and Dry

Meaning: To be left in a difficult or helpless situation without support.

Origin: This idiom originates from the nautical world, where a ship left "high and dry" is stranded on the shore, no longer in the water. The phrase has been used since at least the early 19th century to describe being abandoned or left without help in a difficult situation.

Example: When the funding was cut, the project team was left high and dry.

To Blackball

Meaning: To exclude or vote against someone, especially from a group or organization.

Origin: The phrase "to blackball" originates from a traditional voting system where members of a club or organization used black and white balls to vote secretly on a candidate's membership. A black ball indicated a negative vote. If a candidate received even one black ball, they were rejected. The phrase has been in use since at least the 18th century.

Example: They tried to join the club, but were blackballed by the committee.

To Bury the Hatchet

Meaning: To make peace or resolve a conflict.

Origin: This idiom originates from a Native American practice where, during peace negotiations, tribes would literally bury their weapons as a symbolic act of ending hostilities. The phrase has been used in English since the 17th century to signify making peace or resolving disputes.

Example: After years of rivalry, the two neighbors finally decided to bury the hatchet.

To Give the Cold Shoulder

Meaning: To deliberately ignore or be unfriendly to someone.

Origin: This idiom originates from the custom of serving unwanted guests cold meat, specifically the shoulder cut, as a way of showing they were not welcome. The phrase has been used in English since the early 19th century to describe intentionally ignoring or snubbing someone.

Example: She gave him the cold shoulder after he didn't invite her to the party.

To Let One's Hair Down

Meaning: To relax and enjoy oneself, especially after a period of hard work or tension.

Origin: This idiom dates back to the 17th century, when women would literally let their hair down at the end of the day as a sign of relaxation and informality. The phrase has since come to mean letting go of inhibitions and enjoying oneself.

Example: After a stressful week at work, she needed to let her hair down and have some fun.

To Pull Someone's Leg

Meaning: To tease or joke with someone in a playful manner.

Origin: The exact origin of this idiom is unclear, but it dates back to at least the late 19th century. It is believed to come from the practice of tripping someone as a prank. The phrase now means to joke with someone or playfully deceive them.

Example: Don't worry, I'm just pulling your leg about the surprise party.

To the Moon and Back

Meaning: An expression of immense love or affection.

Origin: This idiom likely originates from the vast distance to the moon, used as a metaphor for the magnitude of one's love or affection. It has been popularized in children's literature and is often used to express an immeasurable amount of love.

Example: I love you to the moon and back, and there's nothing I wouldn't do for you.

Tongue in Cheek

Meaning: To say something in a humorous or ironic manner, not meant to be taken seriously.

Origin: This idiom likely originates from the practice of pressing one's tongue against the inside of the cheek to stifle laughter or show sarcasm. It has been used since at least the early 19th century. The phrase suggests that the speaker is not serious and that their comments should be understood as humorous or ironic.

Example: His comment about quitting his job was meant to be tongue in cheek.

Toss Up

Meaning: A situation where the outcome is uncertain and could go either way.

Origin: This idiom comes from the practice of tossing a coin to decide between two options. The outcome of a coin toss is always

50/50, making it an equal chance for either result. The phrase has been used since at least the early 19th century to describe any situation with an uncertain outcome.

Example: The election is a toss-up; it could go either way.

Tree Hugger

Meaning: A person who is environmentally conscious and supports conservation efforts.

Origin: This term likely originates from the 1970s and 1980s environmental movements, where activists were known to physically hug trees to protect them from being cut down. The phrase has since been used both positively and negatively to describe someone who is passionate about environmental conservation.

Example: She's a proud tree hugger, always advocating for sustainable practices.

Tug at One's Heartstrings

Meaning: To evoke strong emotions of sympathy, pity, or love.

Origin: This idiom originates from the idea that the heart has strings that can be pulled, much like the strings of a musical instrument, to produce strong emotional responses. The phrase has been used since at least the 16th century to describe something that deeply affects one's emotions.

Example: The movie's touching story really tugged at my heartstrings.

Turn a Blind Eye

Meaning: To deliberately ignore something or pretend not to see it.

Origin: This idiom originates from the early 19th century and is often attributed to the British naval hero Admiral Horatio Nelson, who allegedly used his blind eye to look through a telescope and ignore signals to withdraw from battle. The phrase has since been used to describe any act of willful ignorance.

Example: She turned a blind eye to the company's unethical practices.

Turn the Other Cheek

Meaning: To respond to an injury or insult without retaliating.

Origin: This idiom originates from the Bible, specifically from the teachings of Jesus in the New Testament (Matthew 5:39), where he advises turning the other cheek instead of seeking revenge. The phrase has been used since at least the 16th century to describe a pacifist response to aggression.

Example: Even though he was insulted, he chose to turn the other cheek and not retaliate.

Twist of Fate

Meaning: An unexpected event that significantly changes the course of someone's life.

Origin: This idiom likely originates from the idea of fate or destiny being unpredictable and capable of changing direction suddenly.

It has been used since at least the late 19th century to describe a sudden and unforeseen change in circumstances.

Example: Meeting her on that rainy day was a twist of fate that changed his life forever.

U

Under Siege

Meaning: To be surrounded and under attack, often used metaphorically to describe a person or organization facing intense pressure or criticism.

Origin: This idiom originates from military terminology, where a city or fortress is "under siege" when it is surrounded by enemy forces attempting to capture it. The phrase has been used since at least the 15th century and can now describe any situation where someone is facing overwhelming pressure or adversity.

Example: The company is under siege from competitors trying to take over its market share.

Up the Ante

Meaning: To increase the stakes or demands in a situation.

Origin: This idiom comes from the world of gambling, specifically poker, where "ante" refers to a small initial bet that players must make to participate in a game. "Upping the ante" means raising the stakes or increasing the bet. The phrase has been used since at least the 19th century and now applies to any situation where the level of risk or commitment is increased.

Example: The team decided to up the ante by investing more resources into the project.

Upper Hand

Meaning: To have an advantage or control in a situation.

Origin: This idiom likely originates from a children's game called "hand-over-hand," where the person with the uppermost hand on a stick or rope gains control. The phrase has been used since at least the 18th century to describe having a position of advantage or dominance.

Example: With his experience and skills, he has the upper hand in the negotiation.

Upset the Apple Cart

Meaning: To cause disruption or create problems, especially by spoiling a plan or situation.

Origin: This idiom dates back to the late 18th century and originates from the literal act of overturning a cart full of apples, causing a mess and disruption. The phrase has since been used metaphorically to describe any action that disrupts or spoils a plan.

Example: Her unexpected resignation upset the apple cart and threw the project into chaos.

Us and Them

Meaning: A division or conflict between two groups, often implying a sense of separation or opposition.

Origin: This idiom likely originates from the natural human tendency to categorize people into "us" (those we identify with) and "them" (those we see as different or opposed). The phrase has been used since at least the 19th century to describe social or cultural divisions.

Example: The policy debate has created an 'us and them' mentality within the community.

Use Your Noodle

Meaning: To use your brain or think carefully.

Origin: The word "noodle" has been used as a slang term for "head" or "brain" since at least the early 20th century. "Use your noodle" means to think or use your intelligence.

Example: Come on, use your noodle and solve the problem"

W

Way to Go

Meaning: An expression of encouragement or approval, meaning "well done."

Origin: This idiom has been in use since at least the mid-20th century in American English. It likely originates from sports and competitive contexts where spectators and coaches would encourage participants by saying "way to go" to commend their efforts.

Example: Way to go on completing the project ahead of schedule!

Weight off One's Shoulders

Meaning: A feeling of relief after being freed from a burden or responsibility.

Origin: This idiom evokes the image of carrying a heavy load on one's shoulders and the relief felt when it is removed. It has been in use since at least the early 19th century to describe the sensation of being relieved from stress or worry.

Example: After submitting the final report, I felt a huge weight off my shoulders.

Wet Behind the Ears

Meaning: Inexperienced or new to a particular activity or situation.

Origin: This phrase likely originates from the idea that newborn animals are still wet from the womb and not fully dried off, indicating their newness and inexperience. The idiom has been in use since at least the early 20th century.

Example: He's still wet behind the ears in this industry, but he's learning quickly.

Wet Blanket

Meaning: A person who dampens the enthusiasm or enjoyment of others.

Origin: This idiom comes from the literal use of a wet blanket to extinguish fires. It has been used since at least the mid-19th century to describe someone who spoils the fun or excitement in a social setting.

Example: Don't be such a wet blanket, join us and have some fun!

Win-Win Situation

Meaning: A situation where all parties involved benefit or come out ahead.

Origin: This phrase comes from negotiation and conflict resolution terminology and has been in use since the mid-20th century. It describes outcomes where all parties involved gain positive results.

Example: The partnership turned out to be a win-win situation for both companies.

Wise Beyond One's Years

Meaning: To exhibit wisdom or maturity beyond what is typical for someone of that age.

Origin: This idiom has been used since at least the 19th century and emphasizes the idea that someone shows a level of understanding or prudence that surpasses what is expected for their age.

Example: At just 16, her insights on life are wise beyond her years.

With Bells On

Meaning: To be very eager and enthusiastic, ready to participate.

Origin: This idiom likely originates from the idea of adding bells to a horse's harness to make it more festive and noticeable. It has been in use since at least the early 20th century to describe someone who is eagerly and enthusiastically ready for something.

Example: I'll be at the party with bells on!

Workhorse

Meaning: A person or machine that performs hard work consistently and reliably.

Origin: This idiom comes from the literal use of workhorses, which are known for their strength and endurance in performing labor-intensive tasks. It has been in use since at least the 19th century to describe anyone or anything that is particularly reliable and hardworking.

Example: She's the workhorse of the team, always taking on the toughest tasks.

Worth One's Salt

Meaning: To be competent and deserving of one's pay or position.

Origin: This idiom dates back to ancient times when salt was a valuable commodity and sometimes used as currency. The phrase has been in use since at least the Roman era, where soldiers were often paid in salt, and it indicated their worthiness and value.

Example: Any manager worth their salt knows how to motivate their team.

Wreak Havoc

Meaning: To cause chaos or destruction.

Origin: The phrase "wreak havoc" has been in use since at least the 16th century. "Wreak" comes from the Old English word "wrecan," meaning to avenge or cause, and "havoc" originally referred to pillage and widespread destruction. Together, they mean to create widespread disorder or damage.

Example: The storm wreaked havoc on the coastal towns, leaving many without power.

Y

Yes Man

Meaning: A person who agrees with everything someone says, often to gain favor.

Origin: The term "yes man" dates back to the early 20th century and describes someone who habitually agrees with or supports everything their superior says. It suggests a lack of independent thought and a desire to please others, often to the detriment of honesty.

Example: He never offers his own opinion; he's just a yes man to the boss.

Yoke Around One's Neck

Meaning: A burden or responsibility that is difficult to bear.

Origin: This idiom comes from the literal yoke used to harness oxen or other animals for plowing. The yoke is a heavy wooden crosspiece that is placed on the animal's neck, symbolizing a heavy burden or oppressive responsibility. It has been used metaphorically since at least the 16th century.

Example: The debt became a yoke around his neck, weighing him down.

Z

Zero Hour

Meaning: The scheduled time for the start of an operation or event.

Origin: The term "zero hour" originates from military terminology, where it refers to the time set for the beginning of a military operation. The phrase has been used since at least World War I and now applies to any critical time when an event or operation is set to begin.

Example: We're all set; zero hour for the launch is at midnight.

Zero Tolerance

Meaning: A policy of not allowing any exceptions or leniency.

Origin: The term "zero tolerance" emerged in the late 20th century and is often associated with strict enforcement policies in various contexts, such as schools, workplaces, and law enforcement. It means that any infraction, no matter how minor, will be punished.

Example: The company has a zero tolerance policy for workplace harassment.

Zip One's Lip

Meaning: To stop talking or to keep quiet.

Origin: The expression "zip your lip" originated from the phrase "button your lips", which was used in 1868 when buttons were used to close things. As zippers became more popular, the phrase was changed to "zip your lip", which is short for "zipper your lips". By 1943, "zip your lip" was the more common expression.

Just as zipping up a bag prevents anything from coming out, "zipping one's lip" implies the act of silencing oneself, of restraining from speaking. It's a direct and often humorous way of telling someone to be quiet, to stop talking, or to keep a secret.

The image of a securely zipped bag, with its contents safely contained within, perfectly mirrors the desired outcome of "zipping one's lip" – silence, discretion, and the prevention of any further words from escaping.

Example: "He was about to spill the secret, but she told him to zip his lip."

Made in the USA
Coppell, TX
14 March 2025